You Don't Have to Be

BUDDHIST

to Know

NOTHING

an illustrious collection
of thoughts on naught

CONCEIVED AND EDITED BY

JOAN KONNER

 Prometheus Books

59 John Glenn Drive
Amherst, New York 14228-2119

Published 2009 by Prometheus Books

Inquiries should be addressed to
Prometheus Books
59 John Glenn Drive
Amherst, New York 14228–2119
VOICE: 716–691–0133, ext. 210
FAX: 716–691–0137
WWW.PROMETHEUSBOOKS.COM

13 12 11 10 09   5 4 3 2 1

Library of Congress Cataloging-in-Publication Data

You don't have to be Buddhist to know nothing : an illustrious collection of thoughts on naught / edited by Joan Konner.
     p. cm.
     ISBN 978–1–59102–757–7 (hardcover : alk. paper)
     1. Nothing (Philosophy) I. Konner, Joan.

BD398 .Y68 2009
111'.5—dc22

                                                                  2009021863

Printed in the United States on acid-free paper

CONTENTS

BOOK IV: PUBLIC LIBRARY 75

BOOK V: CONCERT HALL 117

BOOK VI: SCHOOL   131

BOOK VII: MUSEUM   171

PREFACE

By homely gift and hindered Words
The human heart is told
Of Nothing—
"Nothing" is the force
That renovates the World—

—EMILY DICKINSON

The void is waiting for vocabulary.

—EDMOND JABÈS

INTRODUCTION

I *was in Aspen, Colorado, on my first on-location shoot as executive producer for the new season of* Bill Moyers' Journal, *fall 1978 on* PBS. *It was late August, and the green and hay-colored meadows were glorious in the Rockies' radiant light. Moyers was shooting an interview with one of his favorite subjects, the late philosopher Mortimer Adler. This program was to be a conversation on Adler's latest book,* Aristotle for Everybody. *Adler's thesis was that Aristotle, by means of reason and logic, had paved The Way to answer life's most persistent questions about the nature of Truth, Beauty, Goodness, and Happiness. Logic and reason were Aristotle's religion—and Adler's, but with an exception, as revealed in the interview. Adler had taken a leap of faith some years earlier, converting from being Jewish, the religion into which he was born, to becoming a Catholic.*

Leap of faith? That mysterious leap keeps leaping up, in both belief and science. An inexplicable change from this to that! An instantaneous shift from here to there! What is a quantum, anyway? And what is the in-between, the blind spot over which the leap occurs?

Between rolls of film, in a scenic cliché, Adler sat down next to me, on a stone beside a babbling brook. I chatted with him and posed a question that was on my mind:

"How do you reconcile Aristotelian logic with Eastern philosophy and religion, which are based on paradoxical logic?" I asked.

As background and a brief digression, I had in mind the documentary I had produced and written a few years earlier for NBC News *called* The Search for Something Else. *It was a report on the spread of Eastern philosophy and religion to the United States through music: the Beatles, the Beach Boys, and others; and changes of hearts and minds through the practices of Buddhism, Yoga, Transcendental Meditation, and Zen, led by gurus from India, Tibet, Japan, and a few American early adopters. A shift in Western consciousness was taking place, especially among young people.*

"That's easy," Adler answered. "They are wrong! Just try flying from New York to Tokyo based on paradoxical logic."

"Oh," I responded. And then, with respectful hesitation, I added, "I didn't know you could take a plane to the Truth."

The concept of Nothing, in Western thought, is a paradox. We simply cannot accept, no less conceive of, the paradoxical concept that "Nothing exists," given that we learn to think and reason in the Western tradition, which is based on Aristotelian logic. The Age of Reason, the Enlightenment, and the scientific method have trained us to think otherwise—rationally, that is. In the material world, which we inhabit, the very words "Nothing exists" are a contradiction in terms, an oxymoron. We are not conditioned to perceive a contradiction-in-terms as possible, as real, as able to be. Our way of seeing does not admit that something is and is not at the same time. We live in an either/or construct.

Take the notion that we are living and dying at this very moment. We just don't think that way. Either we are healthy and alive; or we are ill and dying, although we know that each day of life brings us closer to our inevitable death. A both/and construct, which some call holistic, is not in our cultural curriculum, except that more and more, Eastern thought and spiritual traditions, which are rooted in paradoxical logic, are being assimilated into Western culture.

In fact, Nothing can and does co-exist with Everything, because everything in the natural world, we are learning, has its equal and opposite force—matter and antimatter; electrons and protons, and so forth. We accept "equal and opposite" because we trust science. We also trust, from science, that Nature abhors a vacuum. If a vacuum occurs, nature rushes in to fill it. But where and what would Nature rush in to fill if there wasn't a vacuum? Without Emptiness there would be no opportunity for something new, or something else, to occur. Where would Something happen? Stars disappearing. Novas appearing. Leaves falling. New leaves growing. One generation dying, another being born. Nothing is the still center of the wheel of life. Nothing is the core of creation. In the dark evanescence between equal and opposite, the Universe ignites.

In a very simple way, *You Don't Have to Be Buddhist to Know Nothing* demonstrates, if nothing else, that Nothing, capital N, exists, simultaneously with Everything, capital E. I capitalize Nothing and Everything because, here, they are abstractions, universals, ideals, as if from an existent archetypal sphere or the Platonic world of Ideas, waves that break into particles on the shore of being. Small "n" nothing, and small "e" everything are the actual nothing and everything, the particulars, the particles of our daily existence. We, prisoners of rational thought—like Adler and many other logically positive philosophers—cannot, or will not, believe that nonbeing coexists with being. Nothing would make Everything spooky, kooky, and irrational, or worse, mystical and New Age.

That is, until you take a leap! A quantum leap? A leap of faith? Is faith rational? Is lack of faith reasonable?

I propose readers consider that there is a vacuum everywhere, all the time, right where we are, here and now, which Nature is rushing to fill with Everything—not just anything, but Everything, everything possible according to the observed laws of nature. If there wasn't Nothing, Everything would be static, paralyzed. There could be no motion between bodies, no music minus silence, no rhythm without pause, no meaning without space between words and sentences, no emptiness out of which new thoughts, new works, might arise. Nature is dynamic. Life is dynamic. We know, or believe we know, that the only constant is change, according to not only science but the wisdom of experience. Without Nothing, Change itself could not be constant.

The human brain had a difficult time conceptualizing Nothing, but once conceived in Hindu thought, Nothing became a necessity. The dictionary says Nothing is a point of reckoning. We find Nothing in science. We find it in Art. We find it in the philosophies of Hegel, Heidegger, Sartre, and Levinas. We find it in the plays of Samuel Beckett. We find it in the poems of Emily Dickinson, Robert Frost, and Rainer Maria Rilke. We couldn't calculate, compose, or create without Nothing. There are books, ancient, old, and new, on the history and evolution of Nothing. Though the idea itches, tickles, and teases the brain, the rational mind imposes a No Entry sign, ordering intellect to Keep Out! Off limits! The mind—or should we say, the Western mindset—will not work that way. The eyes will not see that way. Thus, we balance on the tipping point of denial, and miss the point of it All.

In English, there is only one word for Love, although there are many kinds of love that give shape and meaning to life—from romance and friendship to the love of pets and God. Curiously, there are many words for Nothing, from abyss to zip, among them bupkis, emptiness, nada, naught, nirvana, the void, vacuum, zip, zero, and zilch. According to the dictionary, the definition of Nothing/nothing is that which does not exist; utter insignificance, having no value, no magnitude, unimportant, inert. But then, additional meanings: a mark from which the beginning is measured! How invaluable is that? How invaluable is the long list of dictionary definitions following: in chemistry, physics, and mathematics; music, art, and more? Oddly, not in religion! Religion admits no nothing, no uncertainty, no unknown or unknowable. God appears to fill the Void. The Creator, and creation, out of Nothing, Ex Nihilo.

Nothing explains a lot. I would say Nothing explains Everything. If you picture a graph, it coheres around an Origin, the O,O point. The Origin is the still center where opposites intersect. It is the point of connection, the point of interconnection, the point through which something must pass to fuse with its opposite. It is the zero base of becoming. The Origin is the point where the horizontal and vertical intersect, a hole to create new wholes: Plus and Minus; Positive and Negative; Space and Time; Good and Evil; Grief and Joy; West and East; Mind and Body; Beauty and the Beast. The Origin is where One becomes the Other, a point of fusion, of transformation, the nonexistent existence. The missing point, the blind spot, in our perception is the Origin, the leap between before and after, the non-dimensional dimension, the instantaneous Nothing that is everywhere, all the time, coming into and going out of existence in no time, where the arrow ceases to progress over half the remaining space and pierces the target, where Nothing makes room for Everything. Nothing produces Being.

This collection of quotes brings together, in one portable volume, the thoughts of many well-known, and not so well-known, writers and philosophers, artists and musicians, poets and playwrights, geniuses and jokers, who have explored, feared, confronted, experienced, and played with the presence of Nothing in their lives. They knew Nothing intuitively, subjectively, imaginatively, irrationally, and conceptually, and they possessed the wit and words to express it.

You Don't Have to Be Buddhist to Know Nothing is organized within chapter headings that make the abstract and non-material nature of Nothing more accessible, more user-friendly. Adopting the concrete metaphor of a place, a locus, the book guides the reader through the universe of Nothing, to a land called Nowhere, uncharted until now. Following directions to Nowhere, we discover its geography, its landscape, its climate, and a village with inhabitants of various faiths and feelings; habits and practices; professions and traditions. We meet the occupants in the familiar settings of residence, library, concert hall, school, museum, house of worship, theater, corner bar, cemetery, and more. The verbal snapshots create a coherent work of insight, humor, and wonder, as awesome and mysterious as the material universe itself.

On this journey, we learn that there are those who have despaired about Nothing (Book IV: Chapter 6), and others who have laughed about it (Book VIII: Chapters 1 and 4). We find others who have played hide-and-seek with Nothing (Book III: Chapter 7) and some whose minds are burdened by it, weightless though Nothing may be (Book XI: Chapter 2). Still others encounter Nothing and find bliss (Book VI: Chapter 2). Many see Nothing as death itself (Book XI: Chapter 3), approaching it with dread and denial. Nothing, like death, repels the mind and body. It is the unknown before we were born and the unknowable after we die. But Nothing is also potential (Book I: Chapter 0). Nothing may be primal Power. The Force! The instability that is the opportunity to become! (Book II: Chapter 2.) It is the origin of stories, the dark spark igniting the Word: Genesis, Creation, Heaven, Hell, God, and the Apocalypse (Book IV). Each quote is testimony to the perennial search for the nature of truth, existence, and the ground of being.

You Don't Have to Be Buddhist to Know Nothing fills a need, a vacuum, if you will, in the library of the mind that demonstrates that even if we can't see, feel, or touch it, or even imagine it, Nothing is here, all the time. It haunts us like a ghost. It stalks us like a shadow. We find Nothing in the work of some of our greatest Western thinkers, writers, and artists—William Shakespeare, Friedrich Nietzsche, John Cage, Franz Kafka, Albert Camus, Thomas Merton, and more. All have dared to pass the Stop sign, feeling the force of Nothing, like gravity and levity all at once. This book is a witness to Nothing, even if we cannot apprehend it with the rational mind. Nothing may appear to be imaginary, extraneous, illogical, absurd. Nevertheless, Nothing exists like an open secret.

Listen to Nothing's presence—its manifestation in words and feeling. Once we know Nothing, we know we don't know or didn't know or can't know or will know or will never know. Nothing is where knowing stops. And starts! What Nothing should not be is the Dead End of thinking. Nothing is the other half of Being, of the paradox we call reality. Irrational? Naturally. Perhaps these writers will demonstrate what the mind denies, the Nothing that must be, an immaculate conception, an Absolute, maybe the only absolute, the only certainty, the only constant, that we can never, ever, know.

Why, one might ask, is Nothing important? Because it is an essential part of our existence. The now of Nothing is the opportunity to create and to choose. Nothing holds the power to change your life. As the dictionary says: "Nothing is a point of reckoning." What you make of your Nothing is what you make of your life.

Book I

BEFORE

In which we encounter testimony of the existence of Nothing as a necessary presence.

0.

THE ORIGIN

I beheld the earth, and, lo, it was without form, and void; and the heavens, and they had no light.

—JEREMIAH [4:23], OLD TESTAMENT

One suffices to derive all out of nothing
[Omnibus ex nihilo ducendis sufficit unum].

—GOTTFRIED LEIBNIZ

The nature of our existence hides from us the knowledge of first beginnings which are born of the Nothing.

—BLAISE PASCAL

All things were created out of nothingness and thus their true origin is the "Not."

—MEISTER ECKHART

All evolution is a process of making something out of nothing.

—GEORGE BERNARD SHAW

I begin with nothingness.

—CARL GUSTAV JUNG

Nothing's gonna change my world.

—JOHN LENNON AND PAUL MCCARTNEY

I conceptualize absolute beginnings (which requires a theory of the void).

—ALAIN BADIOU

Every physical object or body has come out of nothing, is surrounded by nothing, and will eventually return to nothing.

—ECKHART TOLLE

I would say, not *Ex nihilo nihil fit*, but, "You can't have something without nothing."

—ALAN WATTS

The ten thousand things under heaven are born of Being, and Being is born from Non-Being.

—LAO TZU

For the world to exist, God, who was everything and everywhere, consented to shrink, to leave a vacant space not inhabited by Himself: it is in this "hole" that the world occurred.

—E. M. Cioran

The essential problem of creation is the problem of nothingness. Not how something can be created out of nothing, but how nothing can be created in order that, on the basis of nothing, something can take *place*.

—Maurice Blanchot

Nothingness (*ayin*) is more existent than all the being of the world.

—David ben Abraham ha-Lavan

Everything in existence is either created or not created; there is no third possibility.... The question "What was there prior to the creation of the world?" admits two valid answers: "Everything that was uncreated" or "the nothing."... Besides our world, there is only the nothing; that nothing is everywhere.

—Otto von Guericke

There was emptiness more profound than the void between the stars, for which there was no here and there and before and after, and yet out of that void the entire plenum of existence sprang forth.

—HEINZ R. PAGELS

The void makes the world turn.

—EDMOND JABÈS

The dignity of Nothing is sufficiently exalted in this: that Nothing is the tenuous stuff from which the world was made.

—HILAIRE BELLOC

Nothing is the end as well as beginning of all things.

—HENRY FIELDING

Book II

HERE GOES NOTHING

*In which we see Nothing as
Becoming and discover a land
called Nowhere.*

1.

IN THE
BEGINNING

In the beginning, when God created the heavens and the earth, the earth was a formless wasteland, and darkness covered the abyss, while a mighty wind swept over the waters.

—GENESIS [1:1–2], OLD TESTAMENT

There was chaos.... There was no shape; nothing moved, there was not even a name for it. But in all this emptiness, Earth and Heaven parted and something emerged between the two.

—THE KOJIKI

Heaven does nothing: its non-doing is its serenity
Earth does nothing: its non-doing is its rest
From the union of these two non-doings
All actions proceed,
All things are made.

  —CHUANG TZU (as interpreted by Thomas Merton)

Indiana Jones: Where'd they go? Into space?
Professor Oxley: Not into space … into the space between
 spaces.

   —*INDIANA JONES AND THE*
   KINGDOM OF THE CRYSTAL SKULL

All things come from nowhere!

  —CHUANG TZU (as interpreted by Thomas Merton)

2.

THE LIGHT AT THE END OF THE TUNNEL

We see nothingness making the world iridescent, casting a shimmer over things.

—Jean-Paul Sartre

It's amazing what doesn't exist in the real world.

—Alan Watts

When nothing shatters, everything can be born.

—K. C. COLE

Between the distant stars we hope to someday reach, we see the interstellar Void unfurl its variegated cloak.

—STEN F. ODENWALD

The light we see is a spark; the spark is a star; the star is a sun; the sun is a universe; the universe is nothing.

—VICTOR HUGO

3.

DIRECTIONS

As I went walking I saw a sign there
And on the sign it said "No Trespassing."
But on the other side it didn't say nothing,
That side was made for you and me.

—WOODY GUTHRIE

What people forget is a journey to nowhere starts with a single step, too.

—CHUCK PALAHNIUK

Curt: Well, where are you going?

Wendy: Nowhere.

Curt: Well, you mind if I come along?

—*AMERICAN GRAFFITI*

I started out wanting to forget, and the void mapped my route.

—EDMOND JABÈS

We're in the middle of nowhere, which is the safest part of nowhere.

—*FUTURAMA*

For he journeyed from silence to silence, and I had no course but to follow.

—HAROLD PINTER

More and more I have the feeling that we are getting nowhere. Slowly, as the talk goes on, we are getting nowhere and that is a pleasure.

—JOHN CAGE

To overpower vertigo—the keeper of the abyss—one must tame it, cautiously.

—PHILIPPE PETIT

For him it was a dark passage which led to nowhere, then to nowhere, then again to nowhere, once again to nowhere, always and forever to nowhere, heavy on the elbows in the earth to nowhere, dark, never any end to nowhere, hung on all time always to unknowing nowhere, this time and again for always to nowhere, now not to be borne once again always and to nowhere, now beyond all bearing up, up, up and into nowhere, suddenly, scaldingly, holdingly all nowhere gone and time absolutely still and they were both there, time having stopped and he felt the earth move out and away from under them.

—ERNEST HEMINGWAY

It is by going down into the abyss
that we recover the treasures of life.

—JOSEPH CAMPBELL

Any road followed precisely to its end leads precisely
nowhere.

—FRANK HERBERT

Only a few arrive at nothing, because the way is long.

—ANTONIO PORCHIA

The Stars are setting and the Caravan
Starts for the Dawn of Nothing—Oh, make haste!

—OMAR KHAYYÁM

4.
THE GEOGRAPHY OF NOWHERE

This is a country whose center is everywhere and whose circumference is nowhere. You do not find it by traveling but by standing still.

—THOMAS MERTON

One sticks one's finger into the soil to tell by the smell in what land one is. I stick my finger into existence—it smells of nothing.

—SØREN KIERKEGAARD

The splendor of Silence—of snow-jeweled hills and of ice.
—INGRAM CROCKETT

The end of the rainbow is a bottomless gulf down which you can fall forever without arriving, and the blue distance is a void pit which can swallow you and all your efforts into its emptiness, and still be no emptier.
—D. H. LAWRENCE

Nothingness is found underfoot, as the ground of everything in the everyday world.
—ROBERT E. CARTER

Early on a difficult climb, especially a difficult solo climb, you constantly feel the abyss pulling at your back.... The siren song of the void puts you on edge.
—JON KRAKAUER

The here-and-now mountain is a tiny piece of a piece
of straw
blown off into emptiness.

—RUMI

Here, no here makes sense. And when a human voice rises
in this non-environment, Presence and Absence battle at
the core of its every word, with Absence winning out.

—GABRIEL BOUNOURE

The sun shone, having no alternative, on the nothing new.

—SAMUEL BECKETT

Simmering, perfumed,
The paths narrowed into the hollow.
And the snares almost effaced themselves—
Zeros, shutting on nothing,

Set close, like birth pangs.

—SYLVIA PLATH

An object may exist, and yet be no where: and I assert, that this is not only possible, but that the greatest part of beings do and must exist after this manner.

—DAVID HUME

On every summit you are on the brink of an abyss.

—STANISLAW J. LEC

For the listener, who listens in the snow,
And, nothing himself, beholds
Nothing that is not there and the nothing that is.

—WALLACE STEVENS

Book III

IN RESIDENCE

*In which we are introduced to the
inhabitants of Nowhere.*

1.

FOYER

I like the door best. You can go in and out of it and still go nowhere.

—ANDY WARHOL

The door to the invisible must be visible.

—RENÉ DAUMAL

Look at this window: it is nothing but a hole in the wall, but because of it the whole room is full of light. So when the faculties are empty, the heart is full of light.

—CHUANG TZU (as interpreted by Thomas Merton)

"What is that noise?"
The wind under the door.
"What is that noise now? What is the wind doing?"
Nothing again nothing.
"Do you know nothing? Do you see nothing?
    Do you remember Nothing?"

—T. S. ELIOT

A stairway to nowhere! I think that's just elegant.

—*THE SEVEN YEAR ITCH*

2.

LIVING ROOM

As I was sitting in my chair

I *knew* the bottom wasn't there,
Nor legs, nor back, but I *just sat*,

Ignoring little things like that.

—HUGHES MEARNS

One's imprisonment is therefore organized as a perfectly ordinary, not over-comfortable form of daily life. Everything looks as if it were made of solid, lasting stuff. But on the contrary it is a life in which one is falling towards an abyss. It isn't visible. But if one closes one's eyes, one can hear its rush and roar.

—FRANZ KAFKA

In very truth the old are almost free, and if it is another way of saying that our lives are empty, well—there are days when emptiness is spacious, and nonexistence elevating.

—FLORIDA SCOTT-MAXWELL

The feelings of my smallness and my nothingness always kept me good company.

—POPE JOHN XXIII

3.

DINNER PARTY

My name is Nobody. That is what I am called by my mother and father and by all my friends.

—HOMER

"We were just discussing a most interesting subject," said the earnest matron. "Dr. Pritchett was telling us that nothing is anything."

—AYN RAND

How commonly do we hear, that such a thing smells or tastes of Nothing? The latter I have heard asserted of a dish compounded of five or six savoury ingredients.

—HENRY FIELDING

I believe silence to be now the only sensible form of expression.

—HENRY BROOKS ADAMS

When you have nothing to say, say nothing.

—CHARLES CALEB COLTON

Only that which is not said is sincere.

—FERNANDO SABINO

Blessed is the man who, having nothing to say, abstains from giving us wordy evidence of the fact.

—GEORGE ELIOT

Despite all these jokes, kisses and embraces, there was still a silence within me that left me suffering and isolated in the heart of the crowd.

—ORHAN PAMUK

Just think of all the spare time that has flown

Straight into nothingness by being filled
With forks and faces.

—PHILIP LARKIN

That silence is one of the great arts of conversation is allowed by Cicero himself, who says, there is not only an art but even an eloquence in it.

—HANNAH MORE

Discovering that one has nothing to say, one seeks a way to say *that*.

—SUSAN SONTAG

I love your silences, they are like mine.

—ANTONIN ARTAUD (as told by Anaïs Nin)

Nothing, my dear and clever colleague, is not your run-of-the-mill nothing, the result of idleness and inactivity, but dynamic, aggressive Nothingness, that is to say, perfect, unique, ubiquitous, in other words Nonexistence, ultimate and supreme.

—STANISLAW LEM

If nothing whatsoever existed, there would be no problem and no answer, and the anxieties even of existential philosophers would be permanently laid to rest.

—P. L. HEATH

I think that we communicate only too well, in our silence, in what is unsaid, and that what takes place is a continual evasion, desperate rearguard attempts to keep ourselves to ourselves.

—HAROLD PINTER

I can't take the noise here, my soul shudders at every sound, I shudder all over, but I can't go off by myself, I'd be terrified to be alone in silence.

—ANTON CHEKHOV

I had a feeling once about Mathematics, that I saw it all— Depth beyond depth was revealed to me—the Byss and the Abyss. I saw, as one might see the transit of Venus—or even the Lord Mayor's Show, a quantity passing through infinity and changing its sign from plus to minus. I saw exactly how it happened and why the tergiversation was inevitable: and how the one step involved all the others.... But it was after dinner and I let it go!

—WINSTON CHURCHILL

4.

EAST ROOM

The actualization of the true self equals the actualization of nothingness.

—Keiji Nishitani

Thirty spokes share the wheel's hub;
It is the center hole that makes it useful.
Shape clay into a vessel;
It is the space within that makes it useful.
Cut doors and windows for a room;
It is the holes which make it useful.
Therefore benefit comes from what is there;
Usefulness from what is not there.

—Lao Tzu

Form is emptiness and the very emptiness is form; emptiness does not differ from form, form does not differ from emptiness; whatever is form, that is emptiness, whatever is emptiness, that is form.

—HEART SUTRA

The Tao is (like) the emptiness of a vessel; and in our employment of it we must be on our guard against all fulness.

—LAO TZU

5.

WEST WING

America is the land of zero. Start from zero, we start from nothing. That's the ideal of America.

—JACOB NEEDLEMAN

America I've given you all and now I'm nothing.

—ALLEN GINSBERG

The only way to understand modern life is to grasp at nothing. Because there it is, at every turn—profound, banal, substantial, inescapable.

—INGRID SCHAFFNER

In the United States there is more space where nobody is than where anybody is. This is what makes America what it is.

—GERTRUDE STEIN

Perhaps the blank faceless abstract quality of our modern architecture is a reflection of the anxiety we feel before the void, a kind of visual static which emanates from the psyche of us all, as if we do not know which way to go.

—NORMAN MAILER

What could be more appropriate to an era of compliant consumer culture than a mirror facing a vacuum?

—INGRID SCHAFFNER

Western man, up to his neck in *things*, objects, and the business of mastering them, recoils with anxiety from any possible encounter with Nothingness and labels talk of it as "negative"—which is to say, morally reprehensible.

—WILLIAM BARRETT

Man has turned his back on silence. Day after day he invents machines and devices that increase noise and distract humanity from the essence of life, contemplation, meditation.... Tooting, howling, screeching, booming, crashing, whistling, grinding, and trilling bolster his ego. His anxiety subsides. His inhuman void spreads monstrously like a gray vegetation.

—JEAN ARP

Donald Trump...is the greatest salesman in the world, but he's selling *nothing*. There is no *there* there. There is a lot of *hair* there.

—ANDY KINDLER

Spoken or printed, broadcast over the ether or on wood pulp, all advertising copy has but one purpose—to prevent the will from ever achieving silence. Desirelessness is the condition of deliverance and illumination. The condition of an expanding and technologically progressive system of mass production is universal craving.

—ALDOUS HUXLEY

Progress is a phony word. You may evolve, but progress, in the sense we use it—that's an unthinkable thing to a real Master. Because with him, everything that is regarded as progress is actually a withering away. He wants less and less. What he's getting down to is nudity. Nothingness. Nothing.

—HENRY MILLER

6.

A ROOM OF ONE'S OWN

As I was going up the stair,
I met a man who wasn't there!
He wasn't there again to-day!
I wish, I *wish* he'd stay away!

—HUGHES MEARNS

It is in sleeping that everyone reveals themselves, because of the silence.

—FERNANDO SABINO

Silence is the universal refuge, the sequel to all dull discourses and all foolish acts, a balm to our every chagrin, as welcome after satiety as after disappointment; that background...remains ever our inviolable asylum, where no indignity can assail, no personality disturb us.

—HENRY DAVID THOREAU

Every time I wake I understand how easy it is to be nothing.

—ANTONIO PORCHIA

The silence depressed me. It wasn't the silence of silence. It was my own silence.

—SYLVIA PLATH

Nothingness is revealed in experience, in more or less the same way that the lining of a kimono is revealed: one can tell that the lining is there by the hang of the garment, by "looking through" the garment as it were.... One sees the unseen, and in the case of nothingness, the "hang" of existence-as-experience itself is the unseen ground of the seen foreground.

—ROBERT E. CARTER

Too often I feel like one crossing an abyss on a narrow plank—a glance round might quite unnerve.

—CHARLOTTE BRONTË

There grows up between our senses and all our perceptions, between the shocks of all things and all their commotions, between all agitations and our resolve, a distance, an interval, a time, a void, a space where everything becomes calm, tempered, dim, silent, slow.

—JOSEPH JOUBERT

It is so profound, so sad; the silence of the room in which one dwells alone. It is not alone the silence that surrounds the body, but the silence around the soul.

—GUY DE MAUPASSANT

7.

THE CHILDREN'S HOUR

Go and do nothing for a while.

—LILLIAN HELLMAN

"What are you doing, Jason."

"Nothing." Jason said.

"Suppose you come over here to do it, then." Father said.

—WILLIAM FAULKNER

I remember a wise old gentleman who used to say, "When children are doing nothing, they are doing mischief."

—HENRY FIELDING

I remember as a teenager when my parents asked what I was up to, I would often say, "um…nothing…" This would drive them crazy, understandably, but for me it was a way to keep secrets, to have a private life and to move through the abyss of childhood.

—CLAUDIA GOULD

There's never enough time to do all the nothing you want.

—BILL WATTERSON

"What I like *doing* best is Nothing."

"How do you do Nothing?" asked Pooh, after he had wondered for a long time.

"Well, it's when people call out at you just as you're going off to do it, What are you going to do, Christopher Robin, and you say, Oh, nothing, and then you go and do it."

"Oh, I see," said Pooh.

"This is a nothing sort of thing that we're doing now."

"Oh, I see," said Pooh again.

"It means just going along, listening to all the things you can't hear, and not bothering."

—A. A. MILNE

8.

IN THE GARDEN

It was dusk, a clear night, and I had come out to listen to nothing.

—Verlyn Klinkenborg

As a boy he had spent many hours under the night sky trying to tally the clusters of pinprick lights with the shapes of bears, bulls, archers, and water carriers. But nothing had ever come of it, and he had felt stupid, as though there were a blind spot in the center of his brain.

—Paul Auster

Of course there is nothing the matter with the stars
It is my emptiness among them
While they drift farther away in the invisible morning

—W. S. MERWIN

9.

REFLECTING POOL

I understand everything and everyone, and am nobody and nothing.

—George Bernard Shaw

To be no part of any body, is to be nothing.

—John Donne

Śūnyatā [emptiness] is the point at which we become manifest in our own suchness as concrete human beings.

—Keiji Nishitani

The deepest you is the nothing side, is the side which you don't know.

—Alan Watts

I also am reduced to nothingness, and I shiver on the brink of the great empty abysses of my inner being, stifled by longing for the unknown, consumed with the thirst for the infinite, prostrate before the ineffable.

—Henri-Frédéric Amiel

In this world, the land of chimeras is the only one worth inhabiting; and such is the nullity of human affairs that, outside the one self-existing Being, the only beautiful thing is that which has no existence at all.

—Jean-Jacques Rousseau

This sense of my own weakness and emptiness [*néant*] comforts me. I feel myself a mere speck of dust lost in space, yet I am part of that endless grandeur which envelopes me. I could never see why that should be cause for despair, since there could very well be nothing at all behind the black curtain.

—GUSTAVE FLAUBERT

I was frightened upon finding myself amid nothingness, a nothing myself. I felt like suffocating, thinking and feeling that everything is nothing, solid nothing.

—GIACOMO LEOPARDI

We are lost between the abyss within us and the boundless horizons outside us.

—ROBERT SMITHSON

I'm Nobody! Who are you?
Are you—Nobody—Too?
Then there's a pair of us!
Don't tell! they'd advertise—you know!

—EMILY DICKINSON

"I am zero, naught, one cipher,"
meditated the symbol preceding the numbers.
"Think of nothing. I am the sign of it.
I am bitter weather, zero.
In heavy fog the sky ceiling is zero.
Think of nowhere to go. I am it.
Those doomed to nothing for today
and the same nothing for tomorrow,
those without hits, runs, errors,
I am their sign and epitaph,
the goose egg : 0 :
even the least of these—that is me."

—CARL SANDBURG

Book IV

PUBLIC LIBRARY

In which we find a vast literature expressing the observation, experience, and inspiration of Nothing.

1.
DICTIONARY OF NOTHING

One could say that "being is the negation of the primordial night of nothingness."

—PAUL TILLICH

NOTHING is the shadow of EVERYTHING.

—MEHER BABA

Nothing is an awe-inspiring yet essentially undigested concept, highly esteemed by writers of a mystical or existential tendency, but by most others regarded with anxiety, nausea, or panic.

—P. L. HEATH

The nothing is the force whereby the something can be manifested.

—ALAN WATTS

Voidness is that which stands right in the middle between this and that.

—BRUCE LEE

Whatever we make of the nothing, we do know it—if only as something we constantly mention in everyday talk. With no hesitation we can even give a "definition" of this very obvious and ordinary nothing that runs unnoticed through our talk: "The nothing is the utter negation of everything that is."

—MARTIN HEIDEGGER

Nothingness is the peculiar possibility of being and its unique possibility.

—Jean-Paul Sartre

Nothing could be more awe-inspiring and majestic than the inconceivable vastness and stillness of space, and yet what is it? Emptiness, vast emptiness.

—Eckhart Tolle

The dimensions of time, the present, future, and past, are only that which is becoming and its dissolution into the differences of being as the transition into nothingness, and of Nothingness as the transition into being. The immediate disappearance of these differences into individuality is the present as now, which is itself only this disappearance of being into nothingness, and of nothingness into being.

—Georg Wilhelm Friedrich Hegel

Today, this is the way we define the vacuum: It is the remnant left over in a volume out of which we have removed everything that can possibly be taken out.

—Henning Genz

Nothingness...in its primary sense...is the matrix or "ether" of primary meaninglessness and is the emptiness which must be experienced in order for meaningful experience to be realized.

—JAMES S. GROTSTEIN

It is not that the Tao is the whole of which yin and yang are halves, but rather the Tao is that Median Emptiness that lies in between the two terms of this alternation, as a pervasive and permanent space to prevent them from hardening into opposites.

—PATRICK LAUDE

Nothingness is viewed as a level of awareness that is the result of the "annihilation of thought."

—RABBI DAVID A. COOPER

NIRVANA, n. In the Buddhist religion, a state of pleasurable annihilation awarded to the wise, particularly to those wise enough to understand it.

—AMBROSE BIERCE

What can go beyond the Nothingness that surrounds infinity? This is *Ein Sof.*

—RABBI DAVID A. COOPER

Nothing is not only nothing. It is also our prison.

—ANTONIO PORCHIA

Void … can be understood as potentiality.

—VICTOR BENNETT

Nothingness is being and being nothingness. … Our limited mind can not grasp or fathom this, for it joins infinity.

—AZRIEL OF GERONA

Consciousness … is total emptiness (since the entire world is outside it).

—JEAN-PAUL SARTRE

NOTHING: 1. A negative which is the reality behind every ghostly affirmation. 2. Something that has density without weight, like a barber's breath.

—Elbert Hubbard

PHILOSOPHY, n. A route of many roads leading from nowhere to nothing.

—Ambrose Bierce

2.

READING ROOM

Isn't that just like nothing? To lie in wait at the very beginning and end of every tale?

—INGRID SCHAFFNER

Ulysses … not only begins and ends in nothingness, but it
consists of nothing but nothingness.

—CARL GUSTAV JUNG

The word "nothing" holds one captive, mentally narcotic.

—TANYA LEIGHTON

Nothing absorbs and confuses the operations of soul and sense; indeed, the experience is so transcendent, that the full resources of the language must be strained merely to suggest it.

—ROBERT MARTIN ADAMS

The stars shone forth…like zero dots…scattered in the sky.

—SUBANDHU

Listen to the nothing. Read the blank.

—EDMOND JABÈS

"You cannot enter here," said Gandalf, and the huge shadow halted. "Go back to the abyss prepared for you! Go back! Fall into the nothingness that awaits you and your Master. Go!"

—J. R. R. TOLKIEN

3.

WRITER'S ROOM

I shall…proceed to shew; first, what Nothing is; secondly, I shall disclose the various kinds of Nothing; and, lastly, shall prove its great dignity, and that it is the end of every thing.

—HENRY FIELDING

There are as many varieties of Nothing as of things, people and attitudes.

—ROBERT MARTIN ADAMS

We see the brightness of a new page
where everything yet can happen.

—RAINER MARIA RILKE

As imagination bodies forth
The forms of things unknown, the poet's pen
Turns them to shapes and gives to airy nothing
A local habitation and a name.

—WILLIAM SHAKESPEARE

When I awoke in the middle of the night, not knowing where I was, I could not even be sure at first who I was; I had only the most rudimentary sense of existence, such as may lurk and flicker in the depths of an animal's consciousness; I was more destitute than the cave-dweller; but then the memory—not yet of the place in which I was, but of various other places where I had lived and might now very possibly be—would come like a rope let down from heaven to draw me up out of the abyss of not-being, from which I could never have escaped by myself.

—MARCEL PROUST

Does not every writer start in the presence of a yawning void, his blank sheet of paper...to fill which he must invoke the teeming phantoms of his imagination?

—ROBERT MARTIN ADAMS

This nonexistent center became the favorite place of my pen, the well of dark where the words came to drink before dying on the page.

—EDMOND JABÈS

Society is held together by our need; we bind it together with legend, myth, coercion, fearing that without it we will be hurled into that void, within which, like the earth before the Word was spoken, the foundations of society are hidden.

—JAMES BALDWIN

In this space between utterance and act, word after word, a chasm begins to open, and for one to contemplate such emptiness for any length of time is to grow dizzy, to feel oneself falling into the abyss.

—PAUL AUSTER

There are those who set out from the blank white page and those rarer persons who end up there. Not without difficulty, for it sometimes takes a lot of scratching to recapture a bit of blank whiteness.

—MARCEL BÉNABOU

What seems beautiful to me, what I should like to write, is a book about nothing, a book dependent on nothing external, which would be held together by the strength of its style, just as the earth, suspended in the void, depends on nothing external for its support; a book which would have almost no subject, or at least in which the subject would be almost invisible, if such a thing is possible.

—GUSTAVE FLAUBERT

The blank white page contains the finest songs.

—MARCEL BÉNABOU

A man who keeps a diary pays
Due toll to many tedious days;
But life becomes eventful—then
His busy hand forgets the pen.
Most books, indeed, are records less
Of fulness than of emptiness.

—WILLIAM ALLINGHAM

4.

IN THE STACKS

4.1 SAMUEL BECKETT

Nothing is more real than nothing.

Every word is like an unnecessary stain on silence and nothingness.

The only way one can speak of nothing is to speak of it as though it were something.

If I could speak and yet say nothing, really nothing?... But it seems impossible to speak and yet say nothing, you think you have succeeded, but you always overlook something.

Is there any reason why that terrible materiality of the word surface should not be capable of being dissolved, like for example the sound surface, torn by enormous pauses, of Beethoven's seventh Symphony, so that through whole pages we can perceive nothing but a path of sounds suspended in giddy heights, linking unfathomable abysses of silence?

In reality I said nothing at all, but I heard a murmur, something gone wrong with the silence.

Time did not cease, that would be asking too much, but the wheel of rounds and pauses did, as Murphy with his head among the armies continued to suck in, through all the posterns of his withered soul, the accidentless One-and-Only, conveniently called Nothing.

There is nothing but what is said. Beyond what is said there is nothing.

4.2 ITALO CALVINO

The story must also work hard to keep up with us, to report a dialogue constructed on the void, speech by speech. For the story, the bridge is not finished: beneath every word there is nothingness.

And so you can see this novel so tightly interwoven with sensations suddenly riven by bottomless chasms, as if the claim to portray vital fullness revealed the void beneath.

The word connects the visible trace with the invisible thing, the absent thing, the thing that is desired or feared, like a frail emergency bridge flung over an abyss.

Every void continues in the void, every gap, even a short one, opens onto another gap, every chasm empties into the infinite abyss.

The kernel of the world is empty, the beginning of what moves in the universe is the space of nothingness, around absence is constructed what exists, at the bottom of the Grail is the Tao.

4.3 E. M. CIORAN

On life's circumference the soul promenades, meeting only itself over and over again, itself and its impotence to answer the call of the Void.

What a pity that "nothingness" has been devalued by an abuse of it made by philosophers unworthy of it!

We are fulfilled only when we aspire to nothing, when we are impregnated by that nothing to the point of intoxication.

One clings to trifles in order not to realize what they conceal, one deceives nothingness by something even more null and void.

The abyss summons us, and we lend an ear.

Contrary to that abstract, false void of the philosophers, the mystics' nothingness glistens with plenitude: delight out of this world, discharge of duration, a luminous annihilation beyond the limits of thought.

4.4 EDMOND JABÈS

Emptiness has been sighted.

Every creature is allotted an acre of void to settle in.

God's silence is the abyss of the word.

Nothing, like all, cannot be divided, being always all or nothing in the infinite of all and of nothing, and nobody will ever succeed in taking its measure.

Silence is no weakness of language.
It is, on the contrary, its strength.
It is the weakness of words not to know this.

All certainty is a seat belt, a way of tying us securely to the void as the flight takes off into space.

Every minute is an apex of nothingness.

The visible ... is not the negation of the invisible, but its perverse expression. The call of the abyss.

From the heat of their first blaze to its battered dying down, our glowing words shall have set bounds to the abyss.

The void voids us. To go toward truth means emptying out.

Any page of writing is a knot of silence unraveled.

The abyss has been looked at.

gness we must love everything in us that
 loves when he loves himself. But we must
love it all for exactly the opposite reason.

Words stand between silence and silence: between the silence of things and the silence of our own being.

Life is not accomplishing some special work but attaining to a degree of consciousness and inner freedom which is beyond all works and attainments. That is my real goal. It implies "becoming unknown and as nothing."

From moment to moment I remember with astonishment that I am at the same time empty and full.

There is a silent self within us whose presence is distu
precisely because it is so silent: it *can't* be spoken.

I looked upon what was nothing. I touched what was
without substance,
and within what was not, I am.

4.6 RUMI

Existence:
this place made from our love for that emptiness!

You've heard descriptions
of the ocean of non-existence.
Try, continually, to give yourself
into that ocean.

Move outside the tangle of fear-thinking.
Live in silence.

Like the moon, without legs, I race through nothingness.

An invisible bird flies over,
but casts a quick shadow.

Dear soul, if you were not friends
with the vast nothing inside,
why would you always be casting your net
into it, and waiting so patiently?

Show me that hidden world
because for me, this world is nothing.

4.7 WILLIAM SHAKESPEARE

And straight am nothing: but whate'er I be,
Nor I nor any man that but man is
With nothing shall be pleased till he be eased
With being nothing.

Now thou art an O without a figure. I am better than thou
art now. I am a Fool. Thou art nothing.

Nothing will come of nothing.

My long sickness
Of health and living now begins to mend,
And nothing brings me all things.

Is this nothing?
Why, then the world and all that's in't is nothing;
The covering sky is nothing; Bohemia nothing;
My wife is nothing; nor nothing have these nothings,
If this be nothing.

Hamlet: Do you think I meant country matters?
Ophelia: I think nothing, my lord.
Hamlet: That's a fair thought to lie between maids' legs.
Ophelia: What is, my lord?
Hamlet: Nothing.

Nothing is
But what is not.

Gratiano speaks an infinite deal of nothing,
more than any man in all Venice.

5.
POET'S CORNER

Poetry makes nothing happen.

—W. H. Auden

A thing of beauty is a joy forever:
Its loveliness increases; it will never
Pass into nothingness.

—John Keats

I have nothing to say and I am saying it and that is poetry as I need it.

—JOHN CAGE

I can connect
Nothing with nothing.

—T. S. ELIOT

I cling to nowhere till I fall—
The Crash of nothing, yet of all—

—EMILY DICKINSON

Go rich in poverty
Go rich in poetry.
This nothingness
Is plenitude.

—MAY SARTON

Who shall tempt with wand'ring feet
The dark unbottomed infinite abyss.

—JOHN MILTON

Like a long-legged fly upon the stream
His mind moves upon silence.

—WILLIAM BUTLER YEATS

Nothing, thou elder brother even to Shade.

—JOHN WILMOT

Everything is made of light even the dark night
The candles whisper
As they draw close to watch
The great nothing hoard its winnings

—CHARLES SIMIC

Nothing exists as a block
and cannot be parceled up.

—KAY RYAN

You cannot solder an Abyss
With Air.

—EMILY DICKINSON

No voice; but oh! the silence sank
Like music on my heart.

—SAMUEL TAYLOR COLERIDGE

Such labour'd nothings, in so strange a style,
Amaze the unlearn'd, and make the learned smile.

—ALEXANDER POPE

6.

NO EXIT

Nothingness lies coiled in the heart of being—like a worm.

—JEAN-PAUL SARTRE

Take a good look at this world, how riddled it is with huge, gaping holes, how full of Nothingness, the Nothingness that fills the bottomless void between the stars, how everything about us has become lined with it, how it darkly lurks behind each shred of matter.

—STANISLAW LEM

In the dark there is emphatically 'nothing' to see, though the very world itself is *still* 'there,' and 'there' *more obtrusively.*

—MARTIN HEIDEGGER

Ultimately, I seek to nominate nothingness and meaninglessness as the most dreaded nadir of human experience. I believe that they constitute the fundamental traumatic state.

—JAMES S. GROTSTEIN

Even as we huddle around our hearths and invent stories to convince ourselves that the cosmos is warm and full and inviting, nothingness stares back at us with empty eye sockets.

—CHARLES SEIFE

Struggle as he might, he could not turn himself to the solid earth, he could not get footing. He was suspended on the edge of a void, writhing. Whatever he thought of, was the abyss—whether it were friends or strangers, or work or play, it all showed him only the same bottomless void, in which his heart swung perishing.

—D. H. LAWRENCE

Nothing was the matter, I'd not answer
If no one asked, for nothing was the point.

—RODNEY JONES

Someday this old shack we call the world will fall apart. How, we don't know, and we don't really care either. Since nothing has real substance, and life is a twirl in the void, its beginning and its end are meaningless.

—E. M. CIORAN

Nothing is so insufferable to man as to be completely at rest, without passions, without business, without diversion, without study. He then feels his nothingness, his forlornness, his insufficiency, his dependence, his weakness, his emptiness.

—BLAISE PASCAL

Monday nothing
Tuesday nothing
Wednesday & Thursday nothing
Friday for a change a little more nothing
Saturday once more nothing

—TULI KUPFERBERG (THE FUGS)

And the Lord said:
Man means nothing, he means less to me
Than the lowliest cactus flower
Or the humblest Yucca tree

—RANDY NEWMAN

The pressure of various vague emotions—the sense of life passing by, a longing for novelty—had forced her to a certain limit, forced her to look behind her—and there she had seen not even an abyss but only a void...chaos without shape.

—IVAN TURGENEV

Must I restrain me, through the fear of strife,
From holding up the nothingness of life?
—GEORGE GORDON BYRON

The search for happiness. . . . It ends, and it always ends, in
the ghastly sense of the bottomless nothingness into which
you will inevitably fall if you strain any further.
—D. H. LAWRENCE

The cradle rocks above an abyss, and common sense tells us
that our existence is but a brief crack of light between two
eternities of darkness.
—VLADIMIR NABOKOV

Let us think this thought in its most terrible form: existence
as it is, without sense or aim, but inevitably returning,
without a finale in nothingness: "the eternal return."
—FRIEDRICH NIETZSCHE

Created and annihilated, created and annihilated—what a waste of time.

—RICHARD P. FEYNMAN

The For-itself, in fact, is nothing but the pure nihilation of the In-itself; it is like a hole of being at the heart of Being.

—JEAN-PAUL SARTRE

The cold eternal shores
That look sheer down
To the dark tideless floods of Nothingness
Where all who know may drown.

—EDWIN ARLINGTON ROBINSON

My eyes are squeezed by this blackness.
I see nothing.

—SYLVIA PLATH

Now, when you are young, you will not notice anything wrong, but later, in a few years' time, you will shut your eyes in horror before the void within you. You will lose the power of vision, and the waves of the world will close over your head.

—Franz Kafka

The world is what it is; men who are nothing, who allow themselves to become nothing, have no place in it.

—V. S. Naipaul

It does not do to be frightened of things about which you know nothing. You are like children. Afraid of the dark.

—Donna Tartt

7.

THE CLASSICS

[True genius] ... is creative and makes all from nothing.

—Jean-Jacques Rousseau

I believe in all that has never yet been spoken.

—Rainer Maria Rilke

His silence is more eloquent than words.

—Thomas Carlyle

The silent organ loudest chants
The master's requiem.

—Ralph Waldo Emerson

Saying nothing ... sometimes says The Most.

—Emily Dickinson

The nothing itself noths.

—Martin Heidegger

For in fact what is man in nature? A Nothing in comparison
with the Infinite, an All in comparison with the Nothing, a
mean between nothing and everything.

—Blaise Pascal

NOTHING contains so much dignity as Nothing.

—Henry Fielding

Blessed is he that expects nothing, for he shall never be disappointed.

—BENJAMIN FRANKLIN

One man's void is another man's plenum.

—ROBERT MARTIN ADAMS

•

Perhaps it is not-being that is the true state, and all our dream of life is without existence.

—MARCEL PROUST

All sins are attempts to fill voids.

—SIMONE WEIL

Who in this world has not felt the power of this: a nothing!

—VICTOR HUGO

Nothingness haunts being.

—Jean-Paul Sartre

Nothing is real.

—John Lennon and Paul McCartney

When you got nothing, you got nothing to lose.

—Bob Dylan

Nothing, like something, happens anywhere.

—Philip Larkin

There is no there there.

—Gertrude Stein

Book V

CONCERT HALL

In which we listen to silence—
the only Nothing
we are able to sense.

3.

SYMPHONIES OF SILENCE

After silence that which comes nearest to expressing the inexpressible is music.

—ALDOUS HUXLEY

This 'silence' of his is bellowing up and down Europe!

—ROBERT BOLT

Silence is the element in which great things fashion themselves together; that at length they may emerge, full-formed and majestic, into the daylight of Life, which they are thenceforth to rule.

—THOMAS CARLYLE

Silence reveals itself in a thousand inexpressible forms: in the quiet of dawn, in the noiseless aspiration of trees towards the sky, in the stealthy descent of night, in the silent changing of the seasons, in the falling moonlight, trickling down into the night like a rain of silence, but above all in the silence of the inward soul.

—MAX PICARD

And in the naked light I saw
Ten thousand people, maybe more
People talking without speaking
People hearing without listening
People writing songs that voices never share
No one dare
Disturb the sound of silence

—PAUL SIMON

Silence is the element in which great things fashion themselves together; that at length they may emerge, full-formed and majestic, into the daylight of Life, which they are thenceforth to rule.

—THOMAS CARLYLE

Silence reveals itself in a thousand inexpressible forms: in the quiet of dawn, in the noiseless aspiration of trees towards the sky, in the stealthy descent of night, in the silent changing of the seasons, in the falling moonlight, trickling down into the night like a rain of silence, but above all in the silence of the inward soul.

—MAX PICARD

And in the naked light I saw
Ten thousand people, maybe more
People talking without speaking
People hearing without listening
People writing songs that voices never share
No one dare
Disturb the sound of silence

—PAUL SIMON

The silence is even louder than the cacophony of the chord.

—DANIEL BARENBOIM

The blues came from nothingness, from want, from desire. And when a man sang or played the blues, a small part of the want was satisfied from the music.

—W. C. HANDY

[John Cage's] *4'33"* is music reduced to nothing, and nothing raised to music. It cannot be heard, and is heard anywhere by anyone at any time. It is the extinction of thought, and has provoked more thought than any other music of the second half of the twentieth century.

—PAUL GRIFFITHS

4.

MOMENTS
OF SILENCE

Silence gives voice to the depths, when they are in play, and to distances, if there are any.

—Georges Gusdorf

All I know is that my life is filled with little pockets of silence. When I put a record on the turntable, for example, there's a little interval—between the time the needle touches down on the record and the time the music actually starts—during which my heart refuses to beat.

—Robert Hellenga

You can listen to silence, Reuven. I've begun to realize that you can listen to silence and learn from it. It has a quality and a dimension all its own.

—CHAIM POTOK

Can you feel the silence?

—VAN MORRISON

The notes I handle no better than many pianists. But the pauses between the notes—ah, that is where the art resides.

—ARTUR SCHNABEL

There are silences and silences.
And this one, I don't like at all.

—*FITZCARRALDO*

Silences structure our music, fill the spaces—point, counterpoint—of rhythm, cadence, phrasing.

—JOHN EDGAR WIDEMAN

Music and silence...combine strongly because music is done with silence, and silence is full of music.

—MARCEL MARCEAU

If speech is worth one sela (a small coin so-called), silence is worth *two*.

—THE TALMUD

Experience teaches that silence terrifies people the most.

—BOB DYLAN

Recall gospel's wordless choruses hummed, moaned, keened, words left far behind as singers strive to reach what's unsayable, the silent pulse of Great Time abiding within the song.

—JOHN EDGAR WIDEMAN

The longest silence is the most pertinent question most pertinently put.

—HENRY DAVID THOREAU

All profound things, and emotions of things are preceded and attended by Silence.

—HERMAN MELVILLE

People want lectures; I give them silence.

—MOTHER MEERA

5.

THE AUDIENCE

That man's silence is wonderful to listen to.

—THOMAS HARDY

There are grammatical errors even in his silence.

—STANISLAW J. LEC

I listened to the silence.

—ORHAN PAMUK

Silence is audible to all men, at all times, and in all places. She is when we hear inwardly, sound when we hear outwardly.

—HENRY DAVID THOREAU

The moments when something new has entered us, something unknown; our feelings grow mute in shy embarrassment, everything in us withdraws, a silence arises, and the new experience, which no one knows, stands in the midst of it all and says nothing.

—RAINER MARIA RILKE

Silence: the sleep of birds.

—EDMOND JABÈS

The art of our time is noisy with appeals for silence.

—SUSAN SONTAG

Book VI

SCHOOL

*Wherein we encounter and study
the many fields and disciplines of
Nothing.*

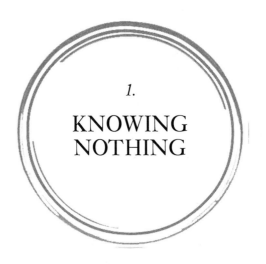

1.

KNOWING NOTHING

The more I read, the more I meditate, and the more I acquire, the more am I enabled to affirm, that I know nothing.

—VOLTAIRE

The only thing that we can know is that we know nothing, and this is the highest flight of human wisdom!

—LEO TOLSTOY

When you know, to know you know. When you don't know, to know you don't know. That's what knowing is.

—CONFUCIUS

"Nothing" can only become a portal into the Unmanifested for you if you don't try to grasp or understand it.

—ECKHART TOLLE

I honestly beleave it iz better tew know nothing than two know what ain't so. [*sic*]

—JOSH BILLINGS

The first and wisest of them all professed
To know this only, that he nothing knew.

—JOHN MILTON

But I cry out to the sky: "I know nothing." And I repeat in a *comical* voice (I cry out to the sky, at times, in this way): "absolutely nothing."

—GEORGES BATAILLE

Become aware of the space that is all around you. Don't think about it. Feel it, as it were. Pay attention to "nothing."

—ECKHART TOLLE

God made everything out of nothing. But the nothingness shows through.

—PAUL VALÉRY

She believed she must now submit to feel that another lesson, in the art of knowing our own nothingness beyond our own circle, was become [*sic*] necessary for her.

—JANE AUSTEN

Ignorance is not just a blank space on a person's mental map. It has contours and coherence, and for all I know rules of operation as well.

—THOMAS PYNCHON

2.

THE JOY OF
UNKNOWING

The mind loves the unknown. It loves images whose meaning is unknown, since the meaning of the mind itself is unknown.

—RENÉ MAGRITTE

The process of delving into the black abyss is to me the keenest form of fascination.

—H. P. LOVECRAFT

It's hard to imagine that nothing at all
could be so exciting could be so much fun
—DAVID BYRNE AND JERRY HARRISON

In writing down my thought, it sometimes escapes me; but this makes me remember my weakness, that I constantly forget. This is as instructive to me as my forgotten thought; for I strive only to know my nothingness.
—BLAISE PASCAL

The unknown was my compass. The unknown was my encyclopedia. The unnamed was my science and progress.
—ANAÏS NIN

For to know nothing is nothing, not to want to know anything likewise, but to be beyond knowing anything, to know you are beyond knowing anything, that is when peace enters in, to the soul of the incurious seeker.
—SAMUEL BECKETT

I felt as though I were floating in space, as though I were safe in the womb of the universe—in a tremendous void, but filled with the highest possible feeling of happiness. "This is eternal bliss," I thought. "This cannot be described; it is far too wonderful!"

—CARL GUSTAV JUNG

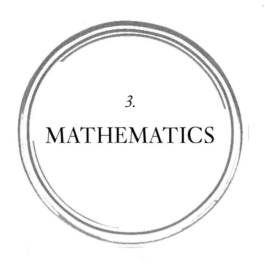

3.
MATHEMATICS

Among the great things which are found among us the existence of Nothing is the greatest.

—Leonardo da Vinci

If you look at zero you see nothing; but look through it and you will see the world.

—Robert Kaplan

The finite is annihilated in the presence of the infinite, and becomes a pure nothing.

—Blaise Pascal

For the great mystery of zero is that it escaped even the Greeks.

—Constance Reid

For good and for ill, the invention of zero let the genie—and also the genius—out of the bottle.

—K. C. Cole

The zero is something that must be there in order to say that nothing is there.

—Karl Menninger

When *sunya* [zero] is added to a number or subtracted from a number, the number remains unchanged; and a number multiplied by *sunya* becomes *sunya*.

—BRAHMAGUPTA

You know the formula: *m* over nought equals infinity, *m* being any positive number? Well, why not reduce the equation to a simpler form by multiplying both sides by nought? In which case you have *m* equals infinity times nought. That is to say that a positive number is the product of zero and infinity. Doesn't that demonstrate the creation of the universe by an infinite power out of nothing?

—ALDOUS HUXLEY

Think of one and minus one. Together they add up to zero, nothing, *nada*, *niente*, right? Picture them together, then picture them *separating*—peeling apart.... Now you have something, you have *two* somethings, where once you had nothing.

—JOHN UPDIKE

We start, then, with nothing, pure zero. But this is not the nothing of negation....

The nothing of negation is the nothing of death, which comes second to, or after, everything. But this pure zero is the nothing of not having been born.... It is the germinal nothing, in which the whole universe is involved or foreshadowed.

—CHARLES S. PEIRCE

For even the smallest zero was a great hole of nothingness, a circle large enough to contain the world.

—PAUL AUSTER

The point about zero is that we do not need to use it in the operations of daily life. No one goes out to buy zero fish. It is in a way the most civilized of all the cardinals, and its use is only forced on us by the needs of cultivated modes of thought.

—ALFRED NORTH WHITEHEAD

Dividing by zero is the closest thing there is to arithmetic blasphemy.

—WILLIAM DUNHAM

Zero shaped humanity's view of the universe—and of God.

—CHARLES SEIFE

The old Church fathers did everything to keep it out of a world which then revolved around one and its multiples... zero was unthinkable. If it wasn't one of something, it couldn't be allowed.

—SADIE PLANT

The fool hath said in his heart that there is no null set. But if that were so, then the set of all such sets would be empty, and hence, *it* would be the null set.

—WESLEY SALMON

4.

THE ARTS

Art adores a vacuum.

—Roberta Smith

Art consists, in all epochs and in any place, of an integrating, re-linking process between man and his reality, which always departs from a nothingness that is nothing and concludes in another Nothingness that is Everything, an Absolute, as a maximum response and spiritual solution to existence.

—Jorge Oteiza

I think about that "empty" space a lot. That emptiness is what allows for something to actually evolve in a natural way. I've had to learn that over the years—because one of the traps of being an artist is to always want to be creating, always wanting to produce.

—MEREDITH MONK

Don't play what's there. Play what's not there.

—MILES DAVIS (as told by Dave Holland)

I like the idea of making films about ostensibly absolutely nothing. I like the irrelevant, the tangential, the sidebar excursion to nowhere that suddenly becomes revelatory.

—ERROL MORRIS

Of every noble work the silent part is best,
Of all expression, that which cannot be expressed.

—WILLIAM WETMORE STORY

It's only through form that we can realize emptiness.

—JACK KEROUAC

All great masters, in their work, seek that profound void within color and outside time.

—ORHAN PAMUK

I really have nothing to say. But I want to say it just the same.

—8½

5.

SCIENCE
SUTRA

Logic is a carpet laid over an abyss.

—O. B. Hardison Jr.

It can be put this way. If I allow all things to vanish, then according to Newton the Galilean inertial space remains; following my interpretation, however, *nothing* remains.

—Albert Einstein

Quite undeservedly, the ether has acquired a bad name.

—FRANK WILCZEK

The universe is made mostly of dark matter and dark energy, and we don't know what either of them is.

—SAUL PERLMUTTER

Time comes to an end in a black hole.

—STEPHEN HAWKING

If there were not void, things could not move at all; for that which is the property of body, to let and hinder, would be present to all things at all times; nothing therefore could go on, since no other thing would be the first to give way.

—LUCRETIUS

So Einstein was wrong when he said, "God does not play dice." Consideration of black holes suggests, not only that God does play dice, but that he sometimes confuses us by throwing them where they can't be seen.

—STEPHEN HAWKING AND ROGER PENROSE

The vacuum of modern particle theory is a strange place indeed. From an unchanging "void" it has become an active arena out of which particles might be created or into which they might be destroyed . . . The vacuum might even be the "source" of all matter in the universe.

—LAWRENCE M. KRAUSS

The vacuum is truly a 'living Form Void,' pulsating in endless rhythms of creation and destruction.

—FRITJOF CAPRA

In the quantum realm, even nothing never sleeps. Nothing is always up to something. Even when there is absolutely nothing going on, and nothing there to do it.

—K. C. COLE

If you were to travel at the speed of light, it would take you several years to get to the nearest stars in our own Milky Way galaxy; but if you were to go to this hole and enter one side, you'd have to travel for a billion years before you would get to the other side.

—LAWRENCE RUDNICK

True talk of Nothing always remains unfamiliar. It does not allow itself to be made common. It dissolves, to be sure, if one places it in the cheap acid of a merely logical cleverness.

—MARTIN HEIDEGGER

Although atoms are way more than 99.99 percent empty space, I have a real problem in walking through a wall.

—LEON LEDERMAN AND DICK TERESI

The truth is that emptiness is the norm of the universe. It is almost void of matter.

—JOHN STEWART COLLIS

The vacuum is a garbage dump. Einstein freed us from it, now we've got to get rid of it again. Some kid now in junior high school will tell us how.

—LEON LEDERMAN

Whenever it looks like there is 'nothing,' there is never 'nothing' there; it's just the beginning of something else about to happen.

—JOSE RODRIGUEZ, junior high school student

6.

CREATIVE
THINKING

I cannot get rid of the idea that the full is an embroidery on the canvas of the void, that being is superimposed on nothing.

—Henri Bergson

It is not possible to visualize Nothing. One way to gain some idea of that terrible state is through the impossibility of visualizing anything before, after or alongside the universe. Now, since we very much want this visualization, but know it only as one that we can never have, it is an impossibility that we experience, existentially, as an absolute limit.

—GERHARD RICHTER

The value of nothingness is that it dissolves all images and conceptions, including itself.

—DANIEL C. MATT

Your mind is trying to make nothing into something. The moment you make it into something, you have missed it.

—ECKHART TOLLE

Nothingness is not, Nothingness "is made-to-be," ... *The being by which Nothingness comes to the world must be its own Nothingness.*

—JEAN-PAUL SARTRE

But if there is a void above and a void below, a void within and a void without, he who is intent on escaping void has need of a certain imaginative mobility.

—ROBERT MARTIN ADAMS

Under sufficient pressure, something and nothing merge on the far side of the mind.

—TIMOTHY WALSH

In a certain way, "thought" means nothing.

—JACQUES DERRIDA

There is something, without object, without substance—a nothing that is not a nothing, for this nothing is full of murmuring, but of a murmuring that has not been named.

—EMMANUEL LEVINAS

Nothing, in short, is given only in relation to what is, and even the idea of nothing requires a thinker to sustain it.

—P. L. HEATH

From Being to Nothingness. But what is *between* the two opposites? A nothingness more essential than Nothingness itself—the void of an interval that continually hollows itself out and in hollowing itself out becomes distended: the nothing as work and movement.

—MAURICE BLANCHOT

Far from being a quirky sideshow, Nothing is never far from the central plots in the history of ideas.

—JOHN D. BARROW

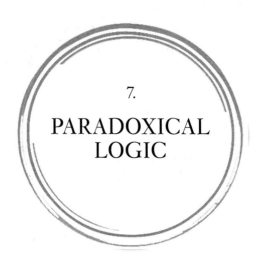

7.

PARADOXICAL LOGIC

Silence, beautiful voice!

—Alfred, Lord Tennyson

Silence is the most powerful cry.

—*Life is Beautiful*

And nothing brings me all things.

—William Shakespeare

Anybody who knows all about nothing knows everything.

—LEONARD SUSSKIND

With the void, full empowerment.

—ALBERT CAMUS

It would seem that the void and the nothingness of the mystics is not a repelling spiritual poverty but an ocean of indescribable wealth, a treasure-house of unearthly beauty. Nothing is all; darkness is light; suffering is joy.

—WILLIAM JOHNSTON

It is when I assent to nothing that I assent to all.

—ANTONIO PORCHIA

Nothingness is the same as fullness. In infinity full is no better than empty. Nothingness is both empty and full.

—CARL GUSTAV JUNG

Nothing satisfies him to whom what is enough is little.

—EPICURUS

Everything had been said in the saying of nothing.

—PAUL GRIFFITHS

Where can I find a man who has forgotten words so that I can have a word with him?

—CHUANG TZU

Being itself is only a pretension of Nothingness.

—E. M. CIORAN

This void is at once the container and the contained.

—JOHN BLOFELD

The Tao in its regular course does nothing (for the sake of doing it), and so there is nothing which it does not do.

—LAO TZU

This is a talk about something and naturally also a talk about nothing. About how something and nothing are not opposed to each other but need each other to keep on going.

—JOHN CAGE

And if you gaze for long into an abyss, the abyss gazes back into you.

—FRIEDRICH NIETZSCHE

Perhaps when we find ourselves wanting everything it is because we are dangerously near to wanting nothing.

—SYLVIA PLATH

To get nowhere you must traverse every known universe: you must be everywhere in order to be nowhere. To have disorder you must destroy *every* form of order. To go mad you must have a terrific accumulation of sanities.

—HENRY MILLER

The less a creature thinks he is, the more he bears. And if he thinks he is nothing, he bears everything.

—ANTONIO PORCHIA

Life is either a daring adventure or nothing.

—HELEN KELLER

I am the self which I will be, in the mode of not being it.

—JEAN-PAUL SARTRE

You and Nothingness are one.

—JIDDU KRISHNAMURTI

I'll speak to thee in silence.

—WILLIAM SHAKESPEARE

To reach satisfaction in all
 desire its possession in nothing.
To come to possess all
 desire the possession of nothing.
To arrive at being all
 desire to be nothing.
To come to the knowledge of all
 desire the knowledge of nothing.

—SAINT JOHN OF THE CROSS

8.

MASTER CLASS

Last year when I talked here I made a short talk. That was because I was talking about something; but this year I am talking about nothing and of course will go on talking for a long time.

—JOHN CAGE

Nothing, in its various guises, has been a subject of enduring fascination for millennia.... Nothing has emerged as an unexpectedly pivotal something, upon which so many of our central questions are delicately poised.

—JOHN D. BARROW

The nothing ceases to be the vague opposite of what-is; instead, it is seen to belong to the very being of what-is.

"Pure being and pure nothing are therefore the same." This thesis of Hegel's (Science of Logic, vol. I, Werke III, 78) is quite right.

—MARTIN HEIDEGGER

[Nothing] cannot become an object of knowledge. You can't do a Ph.D. on "nothing."

—ECKHART TOLLE

Every finite thing implies a void, for it is preceded by a void, occupies a void during the term of its existence, and leaves a void when it passes away.... Thus void...is a sort of metaphysical shadow to which finite things are eternally mated.

—VICTOR BENNETT

I tell you everything that's really nothing,
and nothing of what's everything...
So when I'm going through my routine
do not be fooled by what I am saying.
Please listen carefully and try to hear what I am not saying.

—CHARLES C. FINN

"*Sunyata*" is difficult to translate, but it derives from the Sanskrit root "su," which means, among other things, "to be swollen," both like a hollow balloon—and hence, emptiness—and like a pregnant woman. Thus, while *sunyata* may be nothing, and empty, it is also pregnant with possibilities.

—ROBERT E. CARTER

Before Adam chose to bite the apple, Kierkegaard says, there opened in him a yawning abyss; he saw the possibility of his own freedom in the committing of a future act against the background of Nothingness.

—WILLIAM BARRETT

9.

RECESS

With chess, as in literature, you can't fill all the spaces because there would then be no game to play, no story to tell.

—Timothy Walsh

Tennis can't bring itself to use so blunt a thing as the word 'nil' or 'nothing' or 'zero' to record no score. Instead, it retains the antique term 'love,' which has reached us rather unromantically from *l'oeuf*, the French for an egg which represented the round 0 shape of the zero symbol.

—John D. Barrow

What I hated were people doing things:
Bouncing balls, counting, squirming into jeans
When oblivion waited in every ditch.
I could hear black motors not starting up,
And zeros going nowhere, nothing's gang.

—RODNEY JONES

A riddle constructs a zero around something. It frames an absence.

—TIMOTHY WALSH

Do nothing. Whatever happens, happens. Let it come.

—RUPERT THOMSON

Il dolce far niente.
[How sweet is doing nothing].

—ITALIAN APHORISM

The more exquisitely and delightfully you can do nothing, the higher your life's achievement.

—ELIZABETH GILBERT

There's nothing wrong with doing nothing.

—NEIL GENZLINGER

Generally speaking anybody is more interesting doing nothing than doing anything.

—GERTRUDE STEIN

[Gertrude] Stein was a…master in the art of making nothing happen very slowly.

—CLIFTON FADIMAN

10.

FINAL EXAM

How far must one go to find Nothing?
—Robert Martin Adams

What happens to the hole when the cheese is gone?
—Bertolt Brecht

Shall I believe I am nothing? Shall I believe I am God?
—Blaise Pascal

Book VII

MUSEUM

Wherein we find images and reflections of the past, present, and future of Nothing.

1.

PERMANENT COLLECTION

He [Georges Braque] did not paint things, he explained, he painted space, and then furnished it.

—ALEX DANCHEV

An empty canvas is a living wonder—far lovelier than certain pictures.

—WASSILY KANDINSKY

Everything vanishes around me, and works are born as if out of the void. Ripe, graphic fruits fall off.

—Paul Klee

I believe that what we don't yet know about Nothingness is necessary.

—René Magritte

A hole can have as much meaning as a solid mass—there is a mystery in a hole in a cliff or hillside, in its depth and shape.

—Henry Moore

2.

THE MODERNS

At present, my paintings are invisible and it is these that I wish to display at my next Paris exhibition at Galerie Iris Clert in a clear and positive manner.

—Yves Klein

Your paintings are like my films—they're about nothing... with precision.

—Michelangelo Antonioni (to Mark Rothko)

I'm an optimist, but about nothing.

—FRANCIS BACON

Rauschenberg was able to make nothing the subject of a painting in a way that Cage would, after him, make nothing the subject of a piece of music. Then everything could enter in.

—VINCENT KATZ

Wherever the blind miniaturist's memories reach Allah there reigns an absolute silence, a blessed darkness and the infinity of a blank page.

—ORHAN PAMUK

Conceptual artist Jonathon Keats has unleashed a creation that threatens to render the "silent mode" of mobile phones obsolete: a silent ringtone.

—YEE HUNG LIM

3.
WARHOL RETROSPECTIVE

If you want to know all about Andy Warhol, just look at the surface of my paintings and films and me, and there I am. There's nothing behind it.

Nothing is exciting, nothing is sexy, nothing is not embarrassing.

Question: If you know life is nothing, then what are you living for?
Warhol: For nothing.

So on the one hand I really believe in empty spaces, but on the other hand, because I'm still making some art, I'm still making junk for people to put in their spaces that I believe should be empty: i.e., I'm helping people *waste* their space when what I really want to do is help them *empty* their space.

The great unfulfilled ambition of my life: my own regular TV show. I'm going to call it *Nothing Special.*

I think about nothing. How it's always in style. Always in good taste. Nothing is perfect.

Empty space is never-wasted space.

When *I'm* there, they tell me, nothing happens. I make nothing happen. Wherever I go.

4.

GALLERY OF
BLIND SPOTS

Nothing exists except against a supposed background of absence.

—Jacques Lacan

No lines or imaginings, no shapes or composing or representings, no visions or sensations or impulses, no symbols or signs or impastos, no decoratings or colorings or picturings, no pleasures or pains, no accidents or ready-mades, no things, no ideas, no relations, no attributes, no qualities— nothing that is not of the essence.

—Ad Reinhardt

There are catalepsies, or a kind of sleepwalking through a number of years, in most lives. Maybe it's in these holes that movement takes place.

—GILLES DELEUZE

"I see nobody on the road," said Alice.
"I only wish *I* had such eyes," the King remarked in a fretful tone. "To be able to see Nobody! And at that distance too! Why, it's as much as *I* can do to see real people, by this light!"

—LEWIS CARROLL

"What do you see?"
"Nothing."
"Recognize it?"

—DOUGLAS ADAMS

I want you to think of the curious sensation of *nothing* that lies behind ourselves. Think of the blank space behind the eyes, about the silence out of which all sound comes, and about empty space, out of which all the stars appear.

—ALAN WATTS

At the bottom of the modern man there is always a great thirst for self-forgetfulness, self distraction;...and therefore he turns away from all those problems and abysses which might recall to him his own nothingness.

—HENRI-FRÉDÉRIC AMIEL

Our greatest pretenses are built up not to hide the evil and the ugly in us, but our emptiness. The hardest thing to hide is something that is not there.

—ERIC HOFFER

We run carelessly to the precipice, after we have put something before us to prevent us seeing it.

—BLAISE PASCAL

What is essential is invisible to the eye.

—ANTOINE DE SAINT-EXUPÉRY

When I draw a circle on the blackboard, people see a ball, a circle, or a ring. But I have drawn a wall with a hole in it. You see?

—ALAN WATTS

Silence is not visible, and yet its existence is clearly apparent.

—MAX PICARD

5.

IN STUDIO

I've said before that every craftsman
searches for what's not there
to practice his craft.

—Rumi

Learn how to draw empty space.

—Robert L. Levers Jr.

One creates from nothing. If you try to create from something you're just changing something. So in order to create something you first have to be able to create nothing.

—Werner Erhard

How I paint it *I do not know myself.* I sit down with a white board before the spot that strikes me, I look at what is before me, I say to myself that that white board must become something.

—Vincent van Gogh

Silence is as full of potential wisdom and wit as the unhewn marble of great sculpture.

—Aldous Huxley

Accept what comes from silence.
Make the best you can of it.
Of the little words that come
out of the silence, like prayers
prayed back to the one who prays,
make a poem that does not disturb
the silence from which it came.

—WENDELL BERRY

All I know about method is that when I am not working I
sometimes think I know something, but when I am working,
it is quite clear that I know nothing.

—JOHN CAGE

The Absolute works with nothing.
The workshop, the materials
are what does not exist.

Try and be a sheet of paper with nothing on it.
Be a spot of ground where nothing is growing,
where something might be planted,
a seed, possibly, from the Absolute.

—RUMI

6.

NOTHING IS BEAUTIFUL

Some lovely glorious nothing did I see.

—JOHN DONNE

I do not know which to prefer,
The beauty of inflections
Or the beauty of innuendoes,
The blackbird whistling
Or just after.

—WALLACE STEVENS

I mean that the idea that such complexity can arise not only out of such simplicity, but probably absolutely out of nothing, is the most fabulous, extraordinary idea.

—DOUGLAS ADAMS

As I continued to fall in the dark void, embraced by the vault of the heavens, I sang to the beauty of the stars and made my peace with the darkness.

—HEINZ R. PAGELS

When I fall into the abyss, I go straight into it, head down and heels up, and I'm even pleased that I'm falling in just such a humiliating position, and for me I find it beautiful.

—FYODOR DOSTOEVSKY

Nothing is richer than precious stones and than gold; nothing is finer than adamant, nothing nobler than the blood of kings; nothing is sacred in wars; nothing is greater than Socrates' wisdom—indeed, by his own affirmation, nothing *is* Socrates' wisdom.

—JEAN PASSERAT

Whereas the beautiful teaches us to see no-thing, the sublime teaches us to *be* no-thing.

—CONOR CUNNINGHAM

So life, lived variously and largely, becomes a work of art only when brought to its beautiful conclusion and is reduced to nothingness in the moment when it arrives at perfection.

—W. SOMERSET MAUGHAM

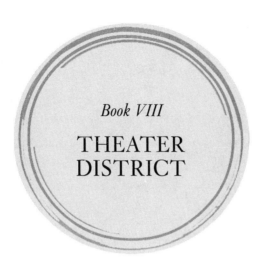

Book VIII

THEATER DISTRICT

*Wherein we witness the masks of
Nothing—and meet them with our
laughter, fear, and tears.*

1.

COMEDY TONIGHT

[*Waiting for Godot*] is a play in which nothing happens, twice.
—Vivian Mercier

Nothing happened.

For a full two minutes nothing continued to happen.
—Douglas Adams

Boris: Nothingness. Nonexistence. Black emptiness.
Sonja: What did you say?
Boris: Oh, I was just planning my future.

—*LOVE AND DEATH*

It's about nothing. . . . Everybody's doing something, we'll do nothing.

—LARRY DAVID

Your shoulders are not that bad. I think I take a bath and slip into nothing more comfortable.

—*THE A-TEAM*

In the beginning there was nothing. God said, "Let there be light!" And there was light. There was still nothing, but you could see it a whole lot better.

—ELLEN DEGENERES

Allan: It's quite a lovely Jackson Pollock, isn't it?

Woman: Yes, it is.

Allan: What does it say to you?

Woman: It restates the negativeness of the universe, the hideous lonely emptiness of existence, nothingness, the predicament of man forced to live in a barren, godless eternity like a tiny flame flickering in an immense void with nothing but waste, horror, and degradation, forming a useless, bleak straightjacket in a black, absurd cosmos.

Allan: What are you doing Saturday night?

Woman: Committing suicide.

—*PLAY IT AGAIN, SAM*

A vacuum is a hell of a lot better than some of the stuff that nature replaces it with.

—TENNESSEE WILLIAMS

2.

MOSTLY MYSTERY

Is it not mysterious that one can know more about things which do not exist than about things which do exist?

—ALFRÉD RÉNYI

Suddenly the Mirror went altogether dark, as dark as if a hole had opened in the world of sight, and Frodo looked into emptiness. In the black abyss there appeared a single Eye that slowly grew, until it filled nearly all the Mirror.... The Eye was rimmed with fire, but was itself glazed, yellow as a cat's, watchful and intent, and the black slit of its pupil opened on a pit, a window into nothing.

—J. R. R. TOLKIEN

Question: If you say my name…I'm not there anymore.
   Who am I?
Answer: Silence!

—*Life is Beautiful*

What if, behind the Nothing, a text were hidden?

—Edmond Jabès

Since the universe does not have an edge, it has no limit;
and since it lacks a limit, it is infinite and unbounded.
Moreover, the universe is infinite both in the number of its
atoms and in the extent of its void.

—Epicurus

The greatest mystery is not that we have been flung at
random between the profusion of matter and of the stars,
but that within this prison we can draw from ourselves
images powerful enough to deny our nothingness.

—André Malraux

3.

IN THE WINGS

I would almost say that the best actor is the man who can do nothing extremely well.

—ALFRED HITCHCOCK

I did change a silence to a pause. It was a rewrite. This silence was a pretty long silence. Now it's a short pause.

—HAROLD PINTER

Nothing happens, nobody comes, nobody goes, it's awful!

—SAMUEL BECKETT

Judging from the plays that are successful these days, maybe
I should write only when I have nothing to say.

—EDWARD ALBEE

One way of looking at speech is to say that it is a constant
stratagem to cover nakedness.

—HAROLD PINTER

I never see a gallery of pictures now but I know how the use
of empty spaces makes a scheme, nor do I ever go to a play
but I see how silence is half the merit of acting and hope
some day for absence and darkness as well upon the stage.

—HILAIRE BELLOC

Silence remains, inescapably, a form of speech (in many instances, of complaint or indictment) and an element in a dialogue.

—Susan Sontag

[Samuel] Beckett could know the difference between a two-seconds of silence and a three-seconds of silence, and he was absolutely right. He was a composer as well as a playwright.

—Edward Albee

Music, commercial breaks, newsflashes, adverts, news broadcasts, movies, presenters—there is no alternative but to fill the screen; otherwise there would be an irremediable void.... That's why the slightest technical hitch, the slightest slip on the part of a presenter becomes so exciting, for it reveals the depth of the emptiness squinting out at us through this little window.

—Jean Baudrillard

4.

THEATER
OF THE
ABSURD

There are now many invisible people on stage.

—Eugène Ionesco

Having found nothing worth more than emptiness, he leaves space vacant.

—Joseph Joubert

A lunatic is a man who sees an abyss and falls into it.

—HONORÉ DE BALZAC

Nobody was to blame. He usually is.

—MARTIN GARDNER

Never get a mime talking. He won't stop.

—MARCEL MARCEAU

In regard to my attempt at the immaterial, which is to say the void...impossible to give you a photograph. Please publish the photocopy, this page written by my own hand, to clearly show that I am of good faith.

—YVES KLEIN

Somewhere a star was going nova, a black hole was vacuuming space, a comet was combing its hair.

—KATE WILHELM

Johnny: And what is it that goes on in this particular post-modernist gas chamber?

Brian: Nothing. It's empty.

Johnny: So what is it that you guard, then?

Brian: Space.

Johnny: You're guarding space? That's stupid, isn't it? Because someone could break in there and steal all the fuckin' space and you wouldn't know where it had gone, would you?

Brian: Good point.

—*NAKED*

You cannot have first space and then things to put into it, any more than you can have first a grin and then a Cheshire cat to fit on to it.

—ALFRED NORTH WHITEHEAD

All my life I give you nothing and still you ask for more.

—GILBERT & GEORGE
(Gilbert Proesch and George Passmore)

Court-martialled in my absence, sentenced to death in my absence. So I said, right, you can shoot me—in my absence.

—Brendan Behan

Life's but a walking shadow, a poor player
That struts and frets his hour upon the stage
And then is heard no more: it is a tale
Told by an idiot, full of sound and fury,
Signifying nothing.

—William Shakespeare

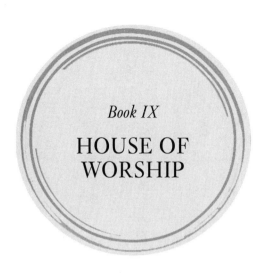

Book IX

HOUSE OF WORSHIP

In which we explore beyond the limits of knowing.

1.

NOTHING IS SACRED

Blessed be nothing.

—RALPH WALDO EMERSON

He [Christ] is an abyss filled with light.

—FRANZ KAFKA

I'm a mystic at bottom and I believe in nothing.

—GUSTAVE FLAUBERT

Silence... belongs to the substance of sanctity. In silence and hope are formed the strength of the Saints (Isaiah, 30:15)

—Thomas Merton

For Shakespeare, in the matter of religion, the choice lay between Christianity and nothing. He chose nothing.

—George Santayana

I am filled with curiosity to behold a man who has the temerity to believe in nothing.

—Ivan Turgenev

People don't so much believe in God as that they choose *not* to believe in nothing.

—Rafael Yglesias

O Mighty Nothing! unto thee,
Nothing, we owe all things that bee.
God spake once, when he all things made,
He sav'd all when he Nothing said.
The world was made of Nothing then;
'Tis made by Nothing now againe.

—RICHARD CRASHAW

Surely it becomes a wise man to regard Nothing with the utmost awe and adoration; to pursue it with all his parts and pains; and to sacrifice to it his ease, his innocence, and his present happiness.

—HENRY FIELDING

Yes, Lord, you are completely innocent; how can You conceive Nothingness, You who are fullness itself? Your presence is light, and changes all into light; how are You to know the twilight of my heart?

—JEAN-PAUL SARTRE

The experience of nothingness is not paralyzing—it is liberating. In its dark light, nothing is beyond questioning, sacred, immobile. On the other hand, since that dark light springs from honesty, courage, freedom, and community, everything in life that promotes these qualities becomes precious and sacred.

—MICHAEL NOVAK

Without God, everything is nothingness; and God? Supreme nothingness.

—E. M. CIORAN

The place of God in my soul is blank.

—MOTHER TERESA

Our awareness of God is a syntax of the silence in which our souls mingle with the divine, in which the ineffable in us communes with the ineffable beyond us.

—ABRAHAM JOSHUA HESCHEL

The Master of all masters
works with nothing.

The more nothing comes into your work,
the more God is there.

—RUMI

He [God] ... exists without existence, and similarly lives
without life, is powerful without power, and knows without
knowledge.

—MAIMONIDES

Nothing contains all things. It is more precious than gold,
without beginning and end, more joyous than the perception of bountiful light, more noble than the blood of
kings, comparable to the heavens, higher than the stars,
more powerful than a stroke of lightning, perfect and
blessed in every way. Nothing always inspires ... Nothing is
everywhere.

—OTTO VON GUERICKE

You do understand, the more dimension, the more nothing, the more infinite, the more nothingness, the more divine, but, inconceivably, we refuse, foolish as we are, to see and contemplate it and to make use of it because it is too dazzling, because it burns reason.

—YVES KLEIN

You come nearer to the apprehension of Him [God]…with every increase in the negations regarding Him.

—MAIMONIDES

The only one who knows, yet without knowing,
is the highest desire, concealed of all concealed, Nothingness.
—ZOHAR (as translated by Daniel C. Matt)

It seemed to a man as though in a dream—it was a waking dream—that he became pregnant with nothing as a woman does with child, and in this nothing God was born; he was the fruit of the nothing. God was born in the nothing.

—MEISTER ECKHART

If there must be a god in the house, let him be one
That will not hear us when we speak: a coolness,

A vermilioned nothingness, any stick of the mass
Of which we are too distantly a part.

—WALLACE STEVENS

Silence alone is respectable and respected. I believe God to
be Silence.

—HENRY BROOKS ADAMS

2.
SEMINARY

Since God's being is incomprehensible and ineffable, the least offensive and most accurate description one can offer is, paradoxically, *nothing*.

—DANIEL C. MATT

God's silence is a more powerful presence than his words.

—GARY HENRY

None preaches better than the ant, and she says nothing.
—BENJAMIN FRANKLIN

Shunyata-shunyata, the emptiness of emptiness, is the final, and in some ways most important, level of voidness. It reminds us that emptiness is in the last analysis itself only an operative concept. It's not just the conditioned that is empty, it's not just the Unconditioned that is empty—but even absolute Emptiness, even the Great Void, is itself empty.

—SANGHARAKSHITA

Ayin is a name for the nameless. It conveys the idea that God is no thing, neither this nor that.... The paradox is that *ayin* embraces "everything" and "nothing."...God is the oneness that is no particular thing, no thingness, Nothingness with a capital N.

—DANIEL C. MATT

In seeing nothing, he [St. Paul] saw the divine Nothing.
—MEISTER ECKHART

He who finds love finds nothing and everything... for he finds a supernatural, supersensual abyss that has no place as its dwelling and finds nothing that can be compared to it. Therefore one compares it with nothing because it is deeper than everything. Therefore it is a nothing to all things because it is incomprehensible.

—JACOB BOEHME

3.

HOUSE OF DOUBT

Nothing exists; all is a dream. God—man—the world—the sun, the moon, the wilderness of stars—a dream, all a dream; they have no existence. *Nothing exists save empty space—and you!*
—MARK TWAIN

Take from the church the miraculous, the supernatural, the incomprehensible, the unreasonable, the impossible, the unknowable, and the absurd, and nothing but a vacuum remains.

—ROBERT G. INGERSOLL

God is a witness that cannot be sworn.

—SAMUEL BECKETT

Religion enables us to ignore nothingness and get on with the jobs of life.

—JOHN UPDIKE

Are we [who have killed God] not plunging continually? Backward, sideward, forward, in all directions? Is there still any up or down? Are we not straying as through an infinite nothing?

—FRIEDRICH NIETZSCHE

The anxiety of emptiness drives us to the abyss of meaninglessness.

—PAUL TILLICH

Perhaps there is no divine book.... This would mean unconditional divine allegiance to a blank book.

—EDMOND JABÈS

If you practice non-doing (*wu wei*), you will have both happiness and well-being.

—CHUANG TZU (as interpreted by Thomas Merton)

The real "doing nothing" implies inner nonresistance and intense alertness.

—ECKHART TOLLE

In silence alone does a man's truth bind itself together and strike root.

—ANTOINE DE SAINT-EXUPÉRY

This is the peace of Buddha, the total silence—because there is nothing to achieve, no one to achieve, nowhere to go, no one to go. Everything empty.

—OSHO

I had the most incredibly mystical experience that challenged every aspect of myself and my life. It was not a momentary thing—there was an inner struggle that went on for days, during which I knew that I had to stop identifying with my ego and my intellect if I was to enter into that transcendent state. I felt on the edge of an abyss, and then on the other side I was sort of re-made, bit by bit, from nothingness into being.

—FRANÇOISE GILOT

Thought shattering itself against its own nothingness is the explosion of meditation.

—JIDDU KRISHNAMURTI

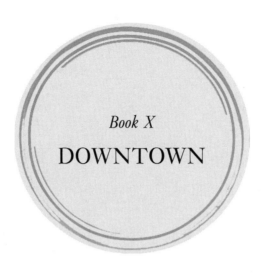

Book X

DOWNTOWN

*Wherein we observe the activities
of the people.*

1.

CITY HALL

The House of Peers throughout the war
Did nothing in particular,
And did it very well.

—W. S. GILBERT AND ARTHUR SULLIVAN

They laboriously do nothing.

—SENECA

As to the future, I rule nothing in or nothing out.

—GEORGE W. BUSH

This is not a personal attack...it's a statement of fact—
Barack Obama has never led anything.
Nothing. Nada.

—RUDOLPH GIULIANI

The sage manages affairs without doing anything, and conveys his instructions without the use of speech.

—LAO TZU

Congress is so strange. A man gets up to speak and says
nothing. Nobody listens—and then everybody disagrees.

—BORIS MARSHALOV

Nothing was ever done so systematically as nothing is being
done now.

—WOODROW WILSON

You are fighting for the biggest nothing in history.

—*APOCALYPSE NOW*

A conference is a gathering of important people who, singly, can do nothing but together can decide that nothing can be done.

—FRED ALLEN

And I? May I say nothing, my lord?

—OSCAR WILDE

It is, no doubt, an immense advantage to have done nothing, but one should not abuse it.

—ANTOINE DE RIVAROL

There are known knowns; there are things we know we know. We also know there are known unknowns; that is to say we know there are some things we do not know. But there are also unknown unknowns—the ones we don't know we don't know.

—DONALD RUMSFELD

I think "no comment" is a splendid expression. I am using it again and again.

—WINSTON CHURCHILL

2.

THE OFFICE

I've never found a way
to hide my doing nothing
day after day

—W. S. Merwin

And I have already achieved a whole year of blissful nothingness, hurrah.

—Arthur C. Clarke

Let me say to you now that to do nothing at all is the most difficult thing in the world, the most difficult and the most intellectual.

—Oscar Wilde

Since my usual technique of pressing on regardless was really no good, this time I'm going to do nothing at all for awhile.

—Ted Hughes

What is left for you to do: to undo yourself in this nothing that you do.

—Maurice Blanchot

This is how the entire course of a life can be changed—by doing nothing.

—Ian McEwan

It takes a lot of time to be a genius, you have to sit around so much doing nothing, really doing nothing.

—GERTRUDE STEIN

Let me tell you, doing nothing is not as easy as it looks. You have to be careful. Because the idea of doing anything, which could easily lead to doing something, that would cut into your nothing, and that would force me to have to drop everything.

—JERRY SEINFELD

Most people spend a good deal of time thinking about nothing.

—JIM HOLT

When you got nothing to do, we can't do it for you.

—LILLIAN HELLMAN

If you have nothing to do please don't do it here.

—CARL SANDBURG

Doing nothing is very hard to do ... you never know when you're finished.

—LESLIE NIELSEN

3.

INN ON
MAIN STREET

He's a real nowhere man,
sitting in his nowhere land,
Making all his nowhere plans for nobody.

—JOHN LENNON AND PAUL MCCARTNEY

I'm an ex-citizen of nowhere. Sometimes I get mighty homesick.

—*PAINT YOUR WAGON*

How stark that life of slouchy avoidance,
Thinking all day and all night of nothing,
Alone in my room with Nietzsche and Sartre.
Nothing is what I'd come from, nowhere
Is where I'd been, and I was nothing's man.

—RODNEY JONES

There are people so near nothing
     they are everywhere without being seen.

—CARL SANDBURG

When the superficial wearies me, it wearies me so much
that I need an abyss in order to rest.

—ANTONIO PORCHIA

I'd rather wake up in the middle of nowhere than in any city
on earth.

—STEVE MCQUEEN

4.

RESTAURANT

Mr. Ping: The secret ingredient is ... nothing!

Po: Huh?

Mr. Ping: You heard me. Nothing! There is no secret ingredient.

Po: Wait, wait ... it's just plain old noodle soup? You don't add some kind of special sauce or something?

Mr. Ping: Don't have to. To make something special you just have to believe it's special.

Po: There is no secret ingredient ...

—*Kung Fu Panda*

5.

CORNER BAR

She would drink so much she would slur her pauses.
—STEVEN WRIGHT

It takes a long time to understand nothing.
—EDWARD DAHLBERG

I collect nothing—with a passion.
—WILLIAM DAVIES KING

Collecting is an attempt to fill the void.

—INGRID SCHAFFNER

I love talking about nothing.... It is the only thing I know anything about.

—OSCAR WILDE

The invisible and nonexistent look very much alike.

—DELOS B. MCKOWN

I did never know so full a voice issue from so empty a heart: but the saying is true, "The empty vessel makes the greatest sound."

—WILLIAM SHAKESPEARE

When we fill the jug, the pouring that fills it flows into the empty jug. The emptiness, the void, is what does the vessel's holding.

—MARTIN HEIDEGGER

A hole is nothing at all, but you can break your neck in it.

—AUSTIN O'MALLEY

I'm nothing, and yet, I'm all I can think about.

—WILLIAM HAMILTON

We have nothing to say to each other. But we don't talk about it.

—ANDRÉ BRIE

One's condition on marijuana is always existential. One can feel the importance of each moment and how it is changing one. One feels one's being, one becomes aware of the enormous apparatus of nothingness—the hum of a hi-fi set, the emptiness of a pointless interruption, one becomes aware of the war between each of us, how the nothingness in each of us seeks to attack the being of others, how our being in turn is attacked by the nothingness in others.

—NORMAN MAILER

6.

WALL STREET

How to live well on nothing a year.

—WILLIAM MAKEPEACE THACKERAY

What's at the end of a million?
000, nothing. Circle with a hole in it.

—*SABRINA*

I got plenty o' nuthin',
An' nuthin's plenty fo' me.

—IRA GERSHWIN AND DUBOSE HEYWARD

In arithmetic as in politics, the importance of one is determined by the number of zeros behind him.

—ANONYMOUS

To whom nothing is given, of him can nothing be required.

—HENRY FIELDING

The impulse to store, on the one hand, and to erase, on the other, is the binary pulse of one and zero. This constitutes the entire language of the computer, a language in which "nought" conveys exactly half of everything written.

—INGRID SCHAFFNER

I worked myself up from nothing to a state of extreme poverty.

—*MONKEY BUSINESS*

Book XI

CITY LIMITS

Wherein our exploration of Nothing arrives at a difficult inconclusion.

1.

THIS WAY OUT

To die would mean nothing else than to surrender a nothing to the nothing, but that would be impossible to conceive, for how could a person, even only as a nothing, consciously surrender himself to the nothing, and not merely to an empty nothing but rather to a roaring nothing whose nothingness consists only in its incomprehensibility.

—Franz Kafka

The hypothesis of absolute void contains nothing at all which terrifies me. I am ready to fling myself into the great black hole with perfect calm.

—GUSTAVE FLAUBERT

Study me then, you who shall lovers be
At the next world, that is, at the next spring;
      For I am a very dead thing,
        In whom Love wrought new alchemy.
          For his art did express
A quintessence even from nothingness,
From dull privations, and lean emptiness;
He ruin'd me, and I am re-begot
Of absence, darkness, death—things which are not.

—JOHN DONNE

On a long enough time line, the survival rate for everyone will drop to zero.

—CHUCK PALAHNIUK

Under all speech that is good for anything there lies a silence that is better. Silence is deep as Eternity; speech is shallow as Time.

—THOMAS CARLYLE

In the end, it will be the Void that survives through the eternities to come, as all the rest of the material world flashes out of existence.

—STEN F. ODENWALD

There is in Nothing something so majestic and so high that it is a fascination and spell to regard it. Is it not that which Mankind, after the great effort of life, at last attains, and that which alone can satisfy Mankind's desire? Is it not that which is the end of so many generations of analysis, the final word of Philosophy, and the goal of the search for reality? Is it not the very matter of our modern creed in which the great spirits of our time repose, and is it not, as it were, the culmination of their intelligence? It is indeed the sum and meaning of all around!

—HILAIRE BELLOC

We are surely doomed to hover continually upon the brink of eternity, without taking a final plunge into the abyss.

—EDGAR ALLAN POE

Perhaps that is the most interesting question of all: to see what happens when there is nothing, and whether or not we will survive that too.

—PAUL AUSTER

Nothingness! To accept the great nothingness of life seemed to be the one end of living.

—D. H. LAWRENCE

2.

TUNNEL
AT THE END
OF THE
LIGHT

At first nothing will happen to us
and later on
it will happen to us again.

—LEONARD COHEN

What did he fear? It was not fear or dread. It was a nothing that he knew too well. It was all a nothing and a man was nothing too. It was only that and light was all it needed and a certain cleanness and order. Some lived in it and never felt it but he knew it all was *nada y pues nada y nada y pues nada*. Our *nada* who art in *nada*, *nada* be thy name thy kingdom *nada* thy will be *nada* in *nada* as it is in *nada*. Give us this *nada* our daily *nada* and *nada* us our *nada* as we *nada* our *nadas* and *nada* us not into *nada* but deliver us from *nada*; *pues nada*. Hail nothing full of nothing, nothing is with thee.

—ERNEST HEMINGWAY

Alas! all is abyss,—action, dream
Desire, speech!

—CHARLES BAUDELAIRE

Behold, ye are of nothing, and your work of nought.

—ISAIAH [41:24], OLD TESTAMENT

He knew that in so far as one denies what is, one is possessed by what is not, the compulsions, the fantasies, the terrors that flock to fill the void.

—URSULA K. LE GUIN

Anxiety is not fear, being afraid of this or that definite object, but the uncanny feeling of being afraid of nothing at all. It is precisely Nothingness that makes itself present and felt as the object of our dread.

—WILLIAM BARRETT

One must not look into the abyss, for in its depths there is an inexpressible charm that draws us down.

—GUSTAVE FLAUBERT

It is his weakness to be proud: he derives, from a comparison of his own extraordinary mind with the dwarfish intellects that surround him, an intense apprehension of the nothingness of human life.

—PERCY BYSSHE SHELLEY

When you see the abyss, and we have looked into it, then what? There isn't much room at the edge—one person, another, not many. If you are there, others cannot be there. If you are there, you become a protective wall. What happens? You become part of the abyss.

—ELIE WIESEL

Nothing can save us from a perpetual headlong fall into a bottomless abyss but a solid footing of dogma; and we no sooner agree to that than we find that the only trustworthy dogma is that there is no dogma.

—GEORGE BERNARD SHAW

Engulfed in the infinite immensity of spaces of which I am ignorant, and which know me not, I am frightened.... The eternal silence of these infinite spaces frightens me.

—BLAISE PASCAL

Some say existence like a Pirouot
And Pirouette, forever in one place,
Stands still and dances, but it runs away;
It seriously, sadly, runs away
To fill the abyss's void with emptiness.

—ROBERT FROST

Silence is all we dread.
There's Ransom in a Voice—
But Silence is Infinity.

—EMILY DICKINSON

Then on the shore
Of the wide world I stand alone, and think
Till love and fame to nothingness do sink.

—JOHN KEATS

To pin your hopes upon the future is to consign those hopes
to a hypothesis, which is to say, a nothingness.

—ANGELA CARTER

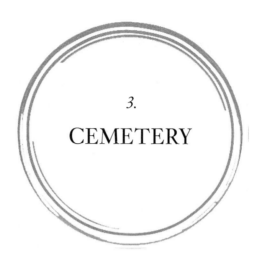

3.

CEMETERY

The dimensions of time, the present, future, and past, are only that which is becoming and its dissolution into the differences of being as the transition into nothingness, and of Nothingness as the transition into being.

—Georg Wilhelm Friedrich Hegel

I like empty spaces that are no longer occupied, although you can tell that people were once there.

—Dick Cole

It's a struggle to understand how at one instant there's something and at the next instant, there's nothing.

—EDWARD "ROCKY" KOLB

A life of nothings, nothing-worth,
From that first nothing ere his birth
To that last nothing under earth!

—ALFRED, LORD TENNYSON

Don't mourn for me now, don't mourn for me never,
For I'm going to do nothing for ever and ever.

—19TH-CENTURY EPITAPH,
Bushey Churchyard, England

Soon there will be nothing where there was never anything.

—SAMUEL BECKETT

Silence precedes us. It knows we will catch up.

—EDMOND JABÈS

We come from a dark abyss, we end in a dark abyss, and we call the luminous interval life.

—Nikos Kazantzakis

After death, said Schopenhauer on the "Today Show," you will be nothing—and you will be everything. He was interrupted by a station break and four commercials and never had a chance to explain the difference.

—Edward Abbey

Dying is not romantic, and death is not a game which will soon be over…Death is not anything…death is not…It's the absence of presence, nothing more…the endless time of never coming back…a gap you can't see, and when the wind blows through it, it makes no sound.

—Tom Stoppard

I placed one foot on the wide plain
of death, and some grand immensity
sounded on that emptiness.

—Rumi

Heaven is a place
A place where nothing
Nothing ever happens

—David Byrne and Jerry Harrison

Nothing was first, and shall be last
for nothing holds for ever,
And nothing ever yet scap't death
So can't the longest liver:
Nothing's so Immortall, nothing can,
From crosses ever keepe a man,
Nothing can live, when the world is gone,
For all shall come to nothing.

—Anonymous

For we brought nothing into this world, and it is certain we
can carry nothing out.

—1 Timothy [6:7], New Testament

This was the abyss to whose brink the music had piped him. To the brink, and now over the brink into this everlasting silence.

—ALDOUS HUXLEY

Silence is the great gratitude when bad music ends.

—CARL SANDBURG

4.

LAST WORDS

Dearest,
Sorry we argued about nothing...

—ALISSA TORRES

There are times when even a fight over nothing means something.

—KENSAKU SEGOE

5.

AFTER LITE

Nothing is too wonderful to be true.

—Michael Faraday

Where every something, being blent together,
Turns to a wild of nothing.

—William Shakespeare

Nothing is the reward of good men who alone can pretend to taste it in long easy sleep, it is the meditation of the wise and the charm of happy dreamers. So excellent and final is it that I would here and now declare to you that Nothing was the gate of eternity, that by passing through Nothing we reached our every object as passionate and happy beings …indeed, indeed when I think what an Elixir is this Nothing I am for putting up a statue nowhere, on a pedestal that shall not exist, and for inscribing on it in letters that shall never be written:

TO NOTHING
THE HUMAN RACE IN GRATITUDE.
—HILAIRE BELLOC

EPILOGUE

There is a here here.

—JOAN KONNER

ACKNOWLEDGMENTS

My deepest gratitude to all who "got" Nothing and who recognized the value of collecting Nothing's pervasive presence in the form of this sound bite history: James Levine, my agent; Steven Mitchell, Editor-in-Chief of Prometheus Books, who understood the potential of this subject; Liel Liebovitz and Diane Nesin, who contributed to the research; Christine Kramer, who managed the production process and the many hidden details therein; Jackie Cooke and Bruce Carle, who designed the book; Vera Aronow, who chased down the clearances. The upfront research credit for Sara Bader is not enough to recognize her full professional and soulful contribution to this project. Thanks always to my husband, Alvin Perlmutter, for his endless supply of encouragement, support, and patience.

BIBLIOGRAPHY

The A-Team. "The A-Team Is Coming, the A-Team Is Coming." Episode 4–14, NBC. Written by Steve Beers. Created by Stephen J. Cannell and Frank Lupo. First broadcast on January 21, 1986.

Abbey, Edward. *The Fool's Progress: An Honest Novel.* New York: Henry Holt, 1988.

Adams, Douglas. *Break the Science Barrier.* Interview by Richard Dawkins, Channel 4. First broadcast in 1996.

Adams, Douglas. *The Ultimate Hitchhiker's Guide to the Galaxy.* New York: Del Rey, 2002.

Adams, Henry. *Letters of Henry Adams.* Edited by Worthington Chauncey Ford. Boston: Houghton Mifflin, 1938.

Adams, Robert Martin. *Nil: Episodes in the Literary Conquest of Void During the Nineteenth Century.* New York: Oxford University Press, 1966.

Albee, Edward. *Conversations with Edward Albee.* Edited by Philip C. Kolin. Jackson: University Press of Mississippi, 1988.

Allen, Fred. "Apology." *Time,* February 5, 1940.

Allingham, William. *William Allingham: A Diary.* Edited by Helen Allingham and Dollie Radford. London: Macmillan, 1907.

American Graffiti. Written by George Lucas, Gloria Katz, and Willard Huyck. Directed by George Lucas. Lucasfilm, 1973.

Amiel, Henri-Frédéric. *Amiel's Journal.* Translated by Mrs. Humphry Ward. London: Macmillan, 1921.

Apocalypse Now. Written by John Milius and Francis Ford Coppola. Directed by Francis Ford Coppola. Hollywood, CA: United Artists, 1979.

Arp, Jean. "Sacred Silence." In *Arp on Arp: Poems, Essays, Memories,* edited by Marcel Jean. Translated by Joachim Neugroschel. New York: Viking Press, 1972.

Auden, W. H. "In Memory of W. B. Yeats." In *Collected Poems,* edited by Edward Mendelson. New York: Modern Library, 2007.

Austen, Jane. *Persuasion.* Introduction by Margaret Drabble. New York: Signet Classic, 1996.

Auster, Paul. "City of Glass." In *The New York Trilogy: City of*

Glass, Ghosts, The Locked Room, introduction by Luc Sante. New York: Penguin, 2006.

———. *In the Country of Last Things*. New York: Viking Press, 1987.

———. *The Invention of Solitude*. New York: Penguin, 1988.

———. *The Music of Chance*. New York: Viking Press, 1990.

Badiou, Alain. *Deleuze: The Clamor of Being*. Translated by Louise Burchill. Minneapolis: University of Minnesota Press, 2000.

Bald, R. C. *John Donne: A Life*. New York: Oxford University Press, 1970.

Baldwin, James. *Notes of a Native Son*. Boston: Beacon Press, 1955.

Barenboim, Daniel. "Master Classes with David Kadouch." *Barenboim on Beethoven*. EMI Classics, 2007.

Barrett, William. *Irrational Man: A Study in Existential Philosophy*. New York: Doubleday, 1958.

Barrow, John D. *Between Inner and Outer Space: Essays on Science, Art, and Philosophy*. New York: Oxford University Press, 2000.

———. *The Book of Nothing*. London: Jonathan Cape, 2000.

Bataille, Georges. *Inner Experience*. Translated and introduction by Leslie Anne Boldt. Albany: State University of New York Press, 1988.

Baudelaire, Charles. "The Gulf." In *The Flowers of Evil*, translated by James McGowan and introduction by Jonathan Culler. New York: Oxford University Press, 1993.

Baudrillard, Jean. *Cool Memories*. Translated by Chris Turner. London: Verso Press, 1990.

Beckett, Samuel. *Disjecta: Miscellaneous Writings and a Dramatic Fragment*. Edited by Ruby Cohn. New York: Grove Press, 1984.

———. *Samuel Beckett: The Grove Centenary Edition*. Edited by Paul Auster. Introduction by Colm Tóibín. 4 Vols. New York: Grove Press, 2006.

———. *Stories & Texts for Nothing*. New York: Grove Press, 1967.

———. *Three Novels: Molloy, Malone Dies, Unnamable*. New York: Grove Press, 1955.

———. *Waiting for Godot: A Tragicomedy in Two Acts*. New York: Grove Press, 1954.

Behan, Brendan. "The Hostage." In *The Complete Plays*, introduction by Alan Simpson. New York: Grove Press, 1978.

Belloc, Hilaire. *On Nothing and Kindred Subjects*. London: Methuen, 1908.

Bénabou, Marcel. *Why I Have Not Written Any of My Books*. Translated by David Kornacker. Lincoln: University of Nebraska Press, 1996.

Bennett, Victor. "The Dowry of Silence." *Music & Letters* 19, no. 1 (January 1938): 61–66.

Bergson, Henri. *Creative Evolution*. Translated by Arthur Mitchell. New York: Henry Holt, 1911.

Berry, Wendell. "How to Be a Poet (To Remind Myself)."

In *Given: New Poems*. Emeryville, CA: Shoemaker and Hoard, 2005.

The Bible: King James Version. Electronic Text Center, University of Virginia. http://etext.virginia.edu/kjv .browse.html.

Bierce, Ambrose. *Devil's Dictionary*. Introduction by Roy Morris Jr. New York: Oxford University Press, 1999.

The Big Nothing. Published in conjunction with the exhibition "The Big Nothing" shown at the Institute of Contemporary Art, in Philadelphia, PA, May 1–August 1, 2004.

Billings, Josh. *Everybody's Friend*. Hartford, CT: American Publishing, 1874.

Blanchot, Maurice. *The Infinite Conversation*. Translated with foreword by Susan Hanson. Minneapolis: University of Minnesota Press, 1993.

———. *The Step Not Beyond*. Translated with an introduction by Lycette Nelson. Albany: State University of New York, 1992.

Boehme, Jacob. *The Way to Christ*. Translated with an introduction by Peter Erb. New York: Paulist Press, 1978.

Bolt, Robert. *A Man for All Seasons: A Play in Two Acts*. London: Heinemann, 1967.

Brecht, Bertolt. *Mother Courage and Her Children: A Chronicle of the Thirty Years' War*. Translated by Eric Bentley. London: Methuen, 1962.

Brockman, John, ed. *What Is Your Dangerous Idea? Today's*

Leading Thinkers on the Unthinkable. New York: Harper Perennial, 2007.

Brontë, Charlotte. *Selected Letters of Charlotte Brontë.* Edited by Margaret Smith. New York: Oxford University Press, 2007.

Brunette, Peter. *The Films of Michelangelo Antonioni.* Cambridge: Cambridge University Press, 1998.

Byers, William. *How Mathematicians Think: Using Ambiguity, Contradiction, and Paradox to Create Mathematics.* Princeton, NJ: Princeton University Press, 2007.

Byron, George Gordon. *Don Juan.* 4 Vols. Austin: University of Texas Press, 1957.

Cage, John. *Silence: Lectures and Writings.* Middletown, CT: Wesleyan University Press, 1961.

Calvino, Italo. *If on a Winter's Night a Traveler.* Translated by William Weaver. New York: Harcourt Brace Jovanovich, 1981.

———. *Six Memos for the Next Millennium.* Cambridge, MA: Harvard University Press, 1988.

———. "Two Tales of Seeking and Losing." In *The Castle of Crossed Destinies*, translated by William Weaver. London: Vintage, 1997.

Campbell, Joseph. *Reflections on the Art of Living: A Joseph Campbell Companion.* Edited by Diane K. Osbon. New York: HarperCollins, 1991.

Capra, Fritjof. *The Tao of Physics: An Exploration of the Parallels between Modern Physics and Eastern Mysticism.* 3rd ed. Boston: Shambhala Publications, 1991.

Carlyle, Thomas. *Critical and Miscellaneous Essays*. Boston: Phillips, Samson, 1859.

———. *The Works of Thomas Carlyle*. Centenary Edition. London: Chapman and Hall, 1901.

Carr, Ian. *Miles Davis: The Definitive Biography*. London: HarperCollins, 1998.

Carroll, Lewis. *Through the Looking-Glass and What Alice Found There*. Edited by Florence Milner. New York: Rand McNally, 1917.

Carter, Angela. *Nights at the Circus*. New York: Penguin, 1986.

Carter, Robert E. "God and Nothingness: Two Sides of the Same Coin?" In *Philosophy of Religion for a New Century: Essays in Honor of Eugene Thomas Long*, edited by Jeremiah Hackett and Jerald Wallulis. Dordrecht, The Netherlands: Kluwer Academic Publishers, 2004.

Chekhov, Anton. "The Cherry Orchard." In *The Complete Plays: Anton Chekhov*, translated and edited by Laurence Senelick. New York: W. W. Norton, 2006.

Chuang Tzu. "External Things." In *The Complete Works of Chuang Tzu*, translated by Burton Watson. New York: Columbia University Press, 1968.

———. *The Way of Chuang Tzu*. Translated and interpreted by Thomas Merton. New York: New Directions, 1969.

Churchill, Winston. *The Churchill Wit*. Edited by Bill Adler. New York: Coward-McCann, 1965.

———. *My Early Life: 1874–1904*. Introduction by William Manchester. New York: Simon & Schuster, 1996.

Cioran, E. M. *All Gall Is Divided.* Translated by Richard Howard. New York: Arcade Publishing, 1999.

————. *Drawn and Quartered.* Translated by Richard Howard. New York: Seaver Books, 1983.

————. *A Short History of Decay.* Translated by Richard Howard. New York: Viking Press, 1975.

————. *Tears and Saints.* Translated by Ilinca Zarifopol-Johnston. Chicago: University of Chicago Press, 1995.

————. *The Temptation to Exist.* Translated by Richard Howard. Introduction by Susan Sontag. Chicago: University of Chicago Press, 1998.

————. *The Trouble with Being Born.* Translated by Richard Howard. New York: Viking Press, 1976.

Clarke, Arthur C. "Quarantine." *Isaac Asimov's Science Fiction Magazine* 1, no. 1 (Spring 1977).

Codrescu, Andrei. *Exquisite Corpse: A Journal of Letters & Life*, no. 4 (April/May 2000). http://www.corpse.org/archives/issue_4/stage_screen/ellis.htm.

Cohen, Leonard. "First of All." In *Book of Longing.* New York: Ecco, 2006.

Cole, Dick. Quoted in "Art Quotes." *The Painter's Keys*, edited by Robert Genn. http://www.painterskeys.com/.

Cole, K. C. *The Hole in the Universe: How Scientists Peered Over the Edge of Emptiness and Found Everything.* New York: Harcourt, 2001.

Coleridge, Samuel Taylor. *The Rime of the Ancient Mariner.*

Edited by H. G. Paul. New York: University Publishing, 1906.

Colie, Rosalie L. *Paradoxia Epidemica: The Renaissance Tradition of Paradox.* Princeton, NJ: Princeton University Press, 1966.

Collis, John Stewart. *Paths of Light.* London: Cassell, 1959.

Colton, Charles Caleb. *Lacon, or, Many Things in Few Words.* London: W. S. Trounce, 1865.

Confucius. *The Analects of Confucius.* Translated by Arthur Waley. New York: Vintage, 1989.

Conze, Edward, trans. *Buddhist Wisdom Books Containing the Diamond Sutra and the Heart Sutra.* London: George Allen and Unwin, 1975.

Cooper, David A. *God Is a Verb: Kabbalah and the Practice of Mystical Judaism.* New York: Riverhead Books, 1997.

Crashaw, Richard. *Steps to the Temple, Delights of the Muses, and Other Poems.* Edited by A. R. Waller. Cambridge: Cambridge University Press, 1904.

Crockett, Ingram. "Orion." In *The Magic of the Woods and Other Poems.* Chicago: Plymouth Publishing, 1908.

Cunningham, Conor. *Genealogy of Nihilism: Philosophies of Nothing and the Difference of Theology.* London: Routledge, 2002.

Dahlberg, Edward. *Reasons of the Heart.* New York: Horizon Press, 1965.

Danchev, Alex. *Georges Braque: A Life.* New York: Arcade Publishing, 2005.

Daumal, René. *Mount Analogue*. Translated by Roger Shattuck. New York: Pantheon Books, 1960.

Deleuze, Gilles. *Negotiations: 1972–1990*. Translated by Martin Joughin. New York: Columbia University Press, 1995.

Derrida, Jacques. *Positions*. Translated and annotated by Alan Bass. Chicago: University of Chicago Press, 1981.

Dickinson, Emily. *The Complete Poems of Emily Dickinson*. Edited by Thomas H. Johnson. New York: Little, Brown, 1960.

———. *The Poems of Emily Dickinson: 3 Volumes in 1*. Edited by Thomas H. Johnson. Cambridge, MA: Belknap Press of Harvard University Press, 1998.

Donne, John. *The Love Poems of John Donne*. Selected and edited by Charles Eliot Norton. Boston: Houghton, Mifflin, 1905.

Dostoevsky, Fyodor. *The Brothers Karamazov*. Translated by Richard Pevear and Larissa Volokhonsky. New York: North Point Press, 1990.

Droit, Roger-Pol. *The Cult of Nothingness: The Philosophers and the Buddha*. Translated by David Streight and Pamela Vohnson. Chapel Hill: University of North Carolina Press, 2003.

Dunham, William. *The Mathematical Universe*. New York: John Wiley & Sons, 1997.

Dylan, Bob. "Like a Rolling Stone." New York: Columbia, 1965.

Eckhart, Meister. "The Love of God." In *Meister Eckhart, from Whom God Hid Nothing: Sermons, Writings, and Sayings*, edited by David O'Neal. Boston: Shambhala Publications, 2005.

———. *Meister Eckhart: Teacher and Preacher*. Edited by Bernard McGinn with the collaboration of Frank Tobin and Elvira Borgstadt. Mahwah, NJ: Paulist Press, 1986.

———. *Sermons and Treatises*. Translated by Maurice O'Connell Walshe. Vol. 1. Dorset, UK: Element Books, 1987.

Eddington, Sir Arthur Stanley. *New Pathways in Science*. Ann Arbor: University of Michigan Press, 1959.

8½. Written by Federico Fellini, Ennio Flaiano, Tullio Pinelli, and Brunello Rondi. Directed by Federico Fellini. Joseph E. Levine, 1963.

Eliot, George. "A Man Surprised at His Originality." In *Impressions of Theophrastus Such: Miscellaneous Essays*. Boston: Estes and Lauriat, 1894.

Eliot, T. S. *The Waste Land*. New York: Boni and Liveright, 1922.

Emerson, Ralph Waldo. *The Complete Works of Ralph Waldo Emerson*. Vol. 9. Boston: Houghton Mifflin, 1904.

———. *Essays by Ralph Waldo Emerson*. Boston: Houghton Mifflin, 1883.

Epicurus. *Letters, Principal Doctrines, and Vatican Sayings*. Translated by Russel M. Greer. New York: Macmillan Publishing, 1964.

Erhard, Werner. *If God Had Meant Man to Fly, He Would Have Given Him Wings, Or: Up to Your Ass in Aphorisms*. San Francisco: Landmark Education, 1973.

Fadiman, Clifton. "Puzzlements." In *Party of One: The Selected Writings of Clifton Fadiman*. Cleveland, OH: World Publishing, 1955.

Faraday, Michael. *Experimental Researches in Chemistry and Physics*. London: Richard Taylor and William Francis, 1859.

Faulkner, William. *The Sound and the Fury*. New York: Vintage, 1984.

Feynman, Richard P. Lecture, University of Southern California, December 6, 1983.

Fielding, Henry. "Essay on Nothing." In *The Works of Henry Fielding*. J. Johnson: London, 1806.

———. *The History of the Adventures of Joseph Andrews, and His Friend Mr. Abraham Adams*. London: George Bell and Sons, 1908.

Finn, Charles C. "Please Hear What I Am Not Saying." *Poetry by Charles C. Finn*. http://www.poetrybycharlesc finn.com.

Fischer, Norman. *Sailing Home*. New York: Free Press, 2008.

Fitzcarraldo. Directed and written by Werner Herzog. New World Pictures, 1982.

Flaubert, Gustave. *The Selected Letters of Gustave Flaubert*. Translated and edited by Francis Steegmuller. New York: Farrar, Straus and Young, 1953.

———. *The Temptation of Saint Antony*. Translated by Kitty Mrosovsky. Ithaca, NY: Cornell University Press, 1981.

Franklin, Benjamin. *Poor Richard's Almanack*. Waterloo, IA: U.S.C. Publishing, 1914.

Frost, Robert. "West-Running Brook." In *The Poetry of Robert Frost*, edited by Edward Connery Lathem. New York: Henry Holt, 1969.

The Fugs. "Nothing." *The Fugs First Album*. Written by Tuli Kupferberg. Washington, DC: Folkways Records, 1965.

Futurama. "Roswell that Ends Well." Episode 4–1, Fox. Written by J. Stewart Burns, Kristine Gore, and Jeff Westbrook. Created by Matt Groening. First broadcast on December 9, 2001.

Gablik, Suzi. *Magritte*. Greenwich, CT: New York Graphic Society, 1970.

Gardner, Martin. *Mathematical Magic Show*. Washington, DC: Mathematical Association of America, 1989.

Geary, James. *Geary's Guide to the World's Greatest Aphorists*. New York: Bloomsbury, 2007.

Genz, Henning. *Nothingness: The Science of Empty Space*. Boston: Perseus Books, 1999.

Genzlinger, Neil. "All Nothing, All the Time." *New York Times*, February 15, 2008.

Gershwin, Ira, and DuBose Heyward. "I Got Plenty O' Nuthin'." In *The Complete Lyrics of Ira Gershwin*, edited by Robert Kimball. New York: Alfred A. Knopf, 1993.

Gilbert, Elizabeth. *Eat, Pray, Love: One Woman's Search for Everything across Italy, India and Indonesia*. New York: Penguin, 2006.

Gilbert, W. S., and Arthur Sullivan. *Iolanthe*. Philadelphia: J. M. Stoddart, 1882.

Ginsberg, Allen. *Journals Mid-Fifties 1954–1958*. Edited by Gordon Ball. New York: HarperCollins, 1995.

Giuliani, Rudolph. Speech at the Republican National Convention, St. Paul, MN, September 3, 2008.

Glueck, Grace. "'Emptying' Sculpture to Make Room for Spiritual Energy." Review of *Oteiza: Myth and Modernism*, Solomon R. Guggenheim Museum. *New York Times*, July 8, 2005.

Goldstein, Amy, and Robert Barnes. "Bush Says He's Not Ruling Out Pardon for Libby." *Washington Post*, July 4, 2007, sec. A04.

Grant, Edward. *Much Ado About Nothing: Theories of Space and Vacuum from the Middle Ages to the Scientific Revolution*. Cambridge: Cambridge University Press, 1981.

"Great 'Cosmic Nothingness' Found." *BBC News*, August 24, 2007, Science & Environment section.

Griffiths, Paul. *Modern Music and After: Directions Since 1945*. 2nd ed. New York: Oxford University Press, 1995.

Grotstein, James S. "Nothingness, Meaninglessness, Chaos and the 'Black Hole.'" *Contemporary Psychoanalysis* 26, no. 2 (April 1990): 257–90.

Gruen, John. "Samuel Beckett Talks About Beckett." *Vogue*, December 1969.

Gusdorf, Georges. *Speaking*. Evanston, IL: Northwestern University Press, 1979.

Gussin, Graham, and Ele Carpenter, eds. *Nothing.* An exhibition catalog. August Media and Northern Gallery of Contemporary Art, 2001.

Gussow, Mel, and Harold Pinter. *Conversations with Pinter.* New York: Grove Press, 1996.

Guthrie, Woody. "This Land Is Your Land." © Copyright 1956 (renewed), 1958 (renewed), 1970 and 1972 Ludlow Music.

Hamilton, William. Cartoon. *New Yorker,* November 24, 2008.

Hardy, Thomas. *Under the Greenwood Tree.* New York: Holt & Williams, 1873.

Harris, Frank. *Bernard Shaw: An Unauthorized Biography Based on First Hand Information.* New York: Simon & Schuster, 1931.

Hawking, Stephen. *The Universe in a Nutshell.* New York: Bantam, 2001.

Hawking, Stephen, and Roger Penrose. *The Nature of Space and Time.* Princeton, NJ: Princeton University Press, 1996.

Heath, P. L. "Nothing." In *The Encyclopedia of Philosophy,* edited by Paul Edwards. Vol. 5. New York: Crowell Collier and Macmillan Publishing, 1967.

Hegel, Georg Wilhelm Friedrich. *The Philosophy of Nature.* Whitefish, MT: Kessinger Publishing, 2004.

Heidegger, Martin. *Being and Time.* Translated by John Macquarrie and Edward Robinson. Foreword by Taylor Carman. New York: Harper Perennial, 2008.

————. *Introduction to Metaphysics*. Translated by Gregory Fried and Richard Polt. New Haven, CT: Yale University Press, 2000.

————. *Poetry, Language, Thought*. Translated by Albert Hofstadter. New York: Perennial Classics, 2001.

————. "What Is Metaphysics?" Translated by Thomas Sheehan. *New Yearbook for Phenomenology and Phenomenological Philosophy*, vol. 1 (2001).

Hellenga, Robert. *The Sixteen Pleasures*. New York: Dell, 1995.

Hellman, Lillian. "The Children's Hour." In *Six Plays by Lillian Hellman*. New York: Modern Library, 1960.

————. *Toys in the Attic*. New York: Dramatists Play Service, 1988.

Hemingway, Ernest. "A Clean, Well-Lighted Place." In *The Complete Short Stories of Ernest Hemingway*. New York: Scribner, 1998.

————. *For Whom the Bell Tolls*. New York: Scribner Classics, 1964.

Henry, Gary. "Story and Silence: Transcendence in the Work of Elie Wiesel." *The Life and Work of Wiesel*. http://www.pbs.org/eliewiesel/life/henry.html.

Herbert, Frank. *Dune*. Radnor, PA: Chilton Book Company, 1965.

Hershon, Paul Isaac, trans. *A Talmudic Miscellany*. Boston: Houghton Mifflin, 1880.

Heschel, Abraham Joshua. *I Asked for Wonder: A Spiritual Anthology*. Chestnut Ridge, NY: Crossroad Publishing, 1983.

————. *Man Is Not Alone.* New York: Farrar, Straus and Giroux, 1951.

Hitchcock, Alfred. "Direction." In *Hitchcock on Hitchcock*, edited by Sidney Gottlieb. Berkeley: University of California Press, 1997.

Hoffer, Eric. *The Passionate State of Mind.* New York: Harper & Row, 1954.

Holt, Jim. "Nothing Ventured." *Harper's Magazine*, November 1994.

The Holy Bible: Containing the Old and New Testaments. New York: Thomas Nelson & Sons, 1903.

Homer. *The Odyssey.* Translated by E. V. Rieu. Revised translation by D. C. H. Rieu. New York: Penguin, 2003.

Hubbard, Elbert. *The Roycroft Dictionary.* East Aurora, NY: Roycrofters, 1914.

Huffington, Arianna. "Picasso: Creator and Destroyer." *Atlantic*, June 1988.

Hughes, Ted. *Letters of Ted Hughes.* Edited by Christopher Reid. London: Faber & Faber, 2007.

Hugo, Victor. *The Toilers of the Sea.* Translated by Graham Robb. New York: Modern Library, 2002.

Hui Hai. *The Zen Teaching of Hui Hai on Sudden Illumination.* Translated by John Blofeld. London: Rider, 1969.

Hume, David. *A Treatise of Human Nature.* Clarendon Press, 1896.

Huxley, Aldous. *Island.* New York: Perennial Classics, 1972.

————. *Point Counter Point.* London: Chatto & Windus, 1928.

———. "The Rest Is Silence." In *Music at Night*. London: Chatto & Windus, 1960.

———. "Silence." In *The Perennial Philosophy*. New York: Perennial Classics, 2004.

I'll Go On: An Afternoon of Samuel Beckett. Film screening and roundtable discussion with Edward Albee, Tom Bishop, Alvin Epstein, Lois Oppenheim, John Turturro. Moderated by Lois Oppenheim. Philoctetes Center, New York, November 22, 2008.

Indiana Jones and the Kingdom of the Crystal Skull. Written by David Koepp. Directed by Steven Spielberg. Lucasfilm, 2008.

Ingersoll, Robert G. "The Ghosts." In *The Works of Robert G. Ingersoll*. Vol. 1. New York: C. P. Farrell, 1900.

Ionesco, Eugène. "The Chairs." In *The Bald Soprano and Other Plays*. New York: Grove Press, 1958.

Isaacson, Walter. *Einstein: His Life and Universe*. New York: Simon & Schuster, 2007.

Izutsu, Toshihiko. *Sufism and Taoism: A Comparative Study of Key Philosophical Concepts*. Berkeley: University of California Press, 1984.

Jabès, Edmond. *The Book of Margins*. Translated by Rosmarie Waldrop. Chicago: University of Chicago Press, 1993.

———. *The Book of Questions II & III*. Translated by Rosmarie Waldrop. Middletown, CT: Wesleyan University Press, 1976.

———. *The Book of Questions IV, V, VI: Yaël, Elya, Aely*. Translated by Rosmarie Waldrop. Middletown, CT: Wesleyan University Press, 1983.

———. *The Book of Questions: El, or the Last Book*. Translated by Rosmarie Waldrop. Middletown, CT: Wesleyan University Press, 1984.

———. *The Book of Resemblances*. Translated by Rosmarie Waldrop. Hanover, NH: University Press of New England, 1990.

———. *The Book of Shares*. Translated by Rosmarie Waldrop. Chicago: University of Chicago Press, 1989.

Janouch, Gustav. *Conversations with Kafka*. Translated by Goronwy Rees. New York: New Directions, 1971.

John XXIII, Pope. "The Text of the Will Left by Pope John XXIII." *New York Times*, June 7, 1963.

John of the Cross. "The Ascent of Mount Carmel." In *John of the Cross: Selected Writings*, edited by Kieran Kavanaugh. Mahwah, NJ: Paulist Press, 1987.

Johnston, William. *Silent Music*. New York: Fordham University Press, 1997.

Jones, Rodney. "Nihilist Time." In *Elegy for the Southern Drawl*. Boston: Houghton Mifflin, 1999.

Jorgensen, Paul A. "Much Ado About Nothing." *Shakespeare Quarterly* 5, no. 3 (Summer 1954): 287–95.

Joubert, Joseph. *The Notebooks of Joseph Joubert*. Translated by Paul Auster. New York: New York Review of Books, 1983.

Jung, Carl Gustav. *Memories, Dreams, Reflections*. Recorded and edited by Aniela Jaffé. Translated by Richard and Clara Winston. New York: Vintage, 1989.

Kafka, Franz. *The Diaries 1910–1923.* Edited by Max Brod. London: Peregrine Books, 1964.

Kandinsky, Wassily. "Empty Canvas, etc." In *The Painter's Object,* edited by Myfanwy Evans, 53–57. New York: Arno Press, 1970.

Kaplan, Robert. *The Nothing That Is: A Natural History of Zero.* New York: Oxford University Press, 1999.

Katz, Vincent. "A Genteel Iconoclasm." *Tate Etc.,* no. 8 (Autumn 2006). http://www.tate.org.uk/tateetc/issue8/erasuregenteel.htm.

Kazantzakis, Nikos. *The Saviors of God: Spiritual Exercises.* Translated by Kimon Friar. New York: Simon & Schuster, 1960.

Keats, John. *The Complete Poems of John Keats.* New York: Modern Library, 1994.

Keller, Helen. *The Open Door.* New York: Doubleday, 1957.

Kerouac, Jack. *The Dharma Bums.* New York: Viking Press, 1958.

Khayyám, Omar. *Rubáiyát of Omar Khayyám.* Translated by Edward Fitzgerald. New York: Thomas Y. Crowell, 1921.

Kierkegaard, Søren. *Repetition: An Essay in Experimenting Psychology by Constantin Constantius.* Translated by H. V. Hong and E. H. Hong. Princeton, NJ: Princeton University Press, 1983.

Kimmelman, Michael. "Old School Bad Boy's Messy World." Review of Francis Bacon retrospective at Tate Britain. *New York Times*, September 24, 2008.

King, William Davies. *Collections of Nothing.* Chicago: University of Chicago Press, 2008.

Kinney, Arthur F., ed. *Classical, Renaissance, and Postmodernist Acts of the Imagination: Essays Commemorating O. B. Hardison Jr.* Newark: University of Delaware Press, 1996.

Klee, Paul. *The Diaries of Paul Klee 1898–1918.* Edited by Felix Klee. Berkeley: University of California Press, 1964.

Klein, Yves. *Overcoming the Problematics of Art: The Writings of Yves Klein.* Translated by Klaus Ottmann. Putnam, CT: Spring Publications, 2007.

Klemesrud, Judy. "A Party for Warhol's 'Folk and Funk.'" *New York Times*, September 20, 1977.

Klinkenborg, Verlyn. "Two Silences." *New York Times*, September 21, 2008.

Krakauer, Jon. "Devils Thumb." In *Testosterone Planet: True Stories from a Man's World.* Palo Alto, CA: Travelers' Tales, 1999.

Krauss, Lawrence M. *The Fifth Essence: The Search for Dark Matter in the Universe.* New York: Basic Books, 1989.

Krishnamurti, Jiddu. *Commentaries on Living.* Wheaton, IL: Theosophical Publishing House, 1967.

———. *Krishnamurti's Notebook.* Bramdean, UK: Krishnamurti Foundation Trust, 2003.

Kung Fu Panda. Written by Jonathan Aibel and Glenn Berger. Directed by Mark Osborne and John Stevenson. Hollywood, CA: Dreamworks Animation and Paramount Pictures, 2008.

Lacan, Jacques. *Écrits*. New York: W. W. Norton, 2002.

Lao Tzu. *Tao Te Ching*. Translated by Gia-Fu Feng and Jane English. New York: Vintage, 1989.

———. *Tao Te Ching*. Sioux Falls, SD: NuVision Publications, 2007.

———. *The Tao Teh King, or the Tao and Its Characteristics*. Translated by James Legge. Project Gutenberg, 1995. http://www.gutenberg.org/dirs/etext95/taote10.txt.

Larkin, Philip. *Collected Poems*. New York: Farrar, Straus and Giroux, 2003.

Laude, Patrick. "God Is the Good." *Parabola: Tradition, Myth, and the Search for Meaning* 33.2 (2008): 16–23.

Lawrence, D. H. *The Fox; The Captain's Doll; The Ladybird*. New York: Penguin Classics, 1994.

———. *Lady Chatterley's Lover*. Edited by Michael Squires. New York: Penguin, 1994.

———. *Women in Love*. Edited by David Farmer, Lindeth Vasey, and John Worthen. New York: Penguin Classics, 2007.

Le Guin, Ursula K. *The Lathe of Heaven*. London: Victor Gollancz Limited, 1979.

Lec, Stanislaw J. *Unkempt Thoughts*. Translated by Jacek Galazka. New York: St. Martin's Press, 1962.

Lederman, Leon, and Dick Teresi. *The God Particle: If the Universe Is the Answer, What Is the Question?* Boston: Mariner Books, 2006.

Lee, Bruce. *Striking Thoughts: Bruce Lee's Wisdom for Daily Living.* Edited by John Little. Boston: Tuttle Publishing, 2000.

Leibniz, Gottfried. *Sämtliche Schriften und Briefe.* Edited by Akademie der Wissenschaften. Series I, vol. 13. Berlin: Akademie Verlag, 1923.

Lem, Stanislaw. "How the World Was Saved." In *The Cyberiad: Fables for the Cybernetic Age,* translated by Michael Kandel. New York: Harcourt Brace Jovanovich, 1985.

Lennon, John, and Paul McCartney. *The Beatles Illustrated Lyrics.* Edited by Alan Aldridge. New York: Delacorte Press, 1969. Lyrics copyright © 1962, 1963, 1964, 1965, 1966, 1967, 1968, 1969 by Northern Songs Limited (London).

Leonardo da Vinci. *The Notebooks of Leonardo da Vinci.* Translated by Edward MacCurdy. New York: Garden City Publishing, 1942.

Leopardi, Giacomo. *Zibaldone: A Selection.* Translated by Martha King and Daniela Bini. New York: Peter Lang, 1992.

Levers, Robert L., Jr. Lecture, University of Texas, Austin, date unknown.

Levinas, Emmanuel. *Alterity and Transcendence.* New York: Columbia University Press, 1999.

Life Is Beautiful. Written by Vincenzo Cerami and Roberto Benigni. Directed by Roberto Benigni. New York: Miramax Films, 1998.

Lim, Yee Hung. "Ringtone? What Ringtone? Conceptual Artist Jonathon Keats, Who Tried to Engineer God in a Lab, Is at It Again with a Phantom Ringtone." *Straits Times* (Indonesia), January 23, 2007.

Love and Death. Written and directed by Woody Allen. Hollywood, CA: United Artists, 1975.

Lovecraft, H. P. *Selected Letters*. Edited by August Derleth and Donald Wandrei. Sauk City, WI: Arkham House, 1971.

Lucretius. *On the Nature of Things*. In *The Stoic and Epicurean Philosophers*, edited by Whitney J. Oates. New York: Modern Library, 1940.

Mailer, Norman. *Cannibals and Christians*. New York: Dell Publishing, 1966.

Maimonides. *The Guide of the Perplexed*. Translated by Shlomo Pines. Vol. 1. Chicago: University of Chicago Press, 1963.

———. *The Guide of the Perplexed*. Translated by Chaim Rabin. Indianapolis, IN: Hackett Publishing, 1995.

Malraux, André. *Anti-Memories*. New York: Holt, Rinehart and Winston, 1968.

Marceau, Marcel. "Speaking Out from Behind the Mask of Mime." *U.S. News & World Report*, February 23, 1987.

Matt, Daniel C. "*Ayin*: The Concept of Nothingness in Jewish Mysticism." In *The Problem of Pure Consciousness:*

Mysticism and Philosophy, edited by Robert K. C. Forman. New York: Oxford University Press, 1990.

————. "Beyond the Personal God." *Ayn Sof Information.* http://www.aynsof.info/Daniel_Matt.htm/.

————. *God & the Big Bang.* Woodstock, VT: Jewish Lights Publishing, 1996.

————. *Zohar: The Book of Enlightenment.* Mahwah, NJ: Paulist Press, 1983.

Maugham, W. Somerset. *A Writer's Notebook.* New York: Penguin, 1984.

Maupassant, Guy de. *Bel-Ami: The History of a Heart.* New York: Pearson Publishing, 1910.

McEwan, Ian. *On Chesil Beach.* New York: Nan A. Talese/ Doubleday, 2007.

McKeen, William. *Rock and Roll Is Here to Stay.* New York: W. W. Norton, 2000.

McQueen, Steve. "The Bad Boy's Breakout." *Life,* July 12, 1963.

Mearns, William Hughes. "Antigonish." In *Best Remembered Poems*, edited by Martin Gardner. New York: Dover Publications, 1992.

Meher Baba. *The Everything and the Nothing.* Beacon Hill, NSW, Australia: Meher House Publications, 1963.

Melville, Herman. *Pierre: Or, The Ambiguities.* New York: Harper & Brothers, 1852.

Menninger, Karl. *Number Words and Number Symbols: A Cultural History of Numbers.* Translated by Paul Broneer. Cambridge, MA: MIT Press, 1969.

Mercier, Vivian. "The Uneventful Event." *Irish Times*, February 18, 1956, p. 6.

Merton, Thomas. *A Book of Hours*. Notre Dame, IN: Sorin Books, 2007.

———. *Thoughts in Solitude*. New York: Farrar, Straus and Giroux, 1999.

Merwin, W. S. *East Window: Poems from Asia*. Port Townsend, WA: Copper Canyon Press, 1998.

———. "In the Winter of My Thirty-Eighth Year." In *Selected Poems*. New York: Atheneum, 1988.

Miller, Henry. *Black Spring*. New York: Grove Press, 1963.

———. *Conversations with Henry Miller*. Edited by Frank L. Kersnowski and Alice Hughes. Jackson: University Press of Mississippi, 1994.

Milne, A. A. "The House at Pooh Corner." In *The World of Pooh*. New York: Dutton, 1957.

Milton, John. *Paradise Lost*. Introduction by John Leonard. New York: Penguin Classics, 2000.

———. "Paradise Regained." In *The Poems of John Milton*. 2 vols. London: Chapman and Hall, 1859.

Monk, Meredith. Interview by *Mountain Record*. http://www.mro.org/mr/archive/22-4/articles/monk.html.

Monkey Business. Written by I. A. L. Diamond, Ben Hecht, and Charles Lederer. Directed by Howard Hawks. Hollywood, CA: Twentieth Century Fox, 1952.

Moore, Henry. *My Ideas, Inspiration and Life as an Artist*. London: Collins & Brown, 1999.

More, Hannah. "Thoughts on Conversation." In *Essays on Various Subjects*. London, 1777.

Morrison, Van. "Summertime in England." *Common One*. Burbank, CA: Warner Brothers, 1980.

Mother Meera. *Mother Meera, Answers Part 1*. Ithaca, NY: Meeramma Publications, 1991.

Mother Teresa. *Come Be My Light: The Private Writings of the Saint of Calcutta*. Edited by Brian Kolodiejchuk, MC. New York: Doubleday, 2007.

Nabokov, Vladimir. *Speak, Memory*. London: Victor Gollancz Limited, 1951.

Naipaul, V. S. *A Bend in the River*. International ed. New York: Vintage, 1989.

Naked. Written and directed by Mike Leigh. Hollywood, CA: Fine Line Features, 1993.

New American Bible. Washington, DC: Confraternity of Christian Doctrine, 1991. http://www.usccb.org/nab/bible/genesis/genesis1.htm.

Newman, Michael, and Jon Bird, eds. *Rewriting Conceptual Art*. London: Reaktion Books, 1999.

Newman, Randy. "God's Song (That's Why I Love Mankind)." *Sail Away*, 2002.

Nielsen, Leslie. Quoted in the Internet Movie Database. http://www.imdb.com/name/nm0000558/bio.

Nietzsche, Friedrich. *The Nietzsche Reader*. Edited by Keith Ansell-Pearson and Duncan Large. Malden, MA: Blackwell Publishing, 2006.

Nin, Anaïs. *The Diary of Anaïs Nin: 1931–1934.* Vol. 1. Edited by Gunther Stuhlmann. New York: Harcourt, 1994.

——. *The Diary of Anaïs Nin: 1944–1947.* Vol. 4. Edited and preface by Gunther Stuhlmann. New York: Harcourt Brace Jovanovich, 1971.

Nishitani, Keiji. *Religion and Nothingness.* Translated by Jan Van Bragt. Berkeley: University of California Press, 1982.

——. *The Religious Philosophy of Nishitani Keiji.* Edited by Taitetsu Unno. Fremont, CA: Asian Humanities Press, 1989.

Novak, Michael. *The Experience of Nothingness.* Revised and expanded ed. New Brunswick, NJ: Transaction Publishers, 1998.

O'Malley, Austin. *Keystones of Thought.* New York: Devin-Adair, 1914.

Oldenwald, Sten F. *Patterns in the Void.* Boulder, CO: Westview Press, 2002.

Osho. *Hsin Hsin Ming: The Book of Nothing.* Madras, OR: Rajneesh Foundation International, 1983.

Pagels, Heinz R. *The Cosmic Code: Quantum Physics as the Language of Nature.* New York: Penguin, 1994.

Paint Your Wagon. Written by Alan Jay Lerner and Paddy Chayefsky based on the musical by Alan Jay Lerner and Frederick Loewe. Directed by Joshua Logan. Hollywood, CA: Paramount Pictures, 1969.

Palahniuk, Chuck. *Fight Club.* New York: W. W. Norton, 1996.

————. *Survivor*. New York: Anchor Books, 2000.

Pamuk, Orhan. *My Name Is Red*. New York: Alfred A. Knopf, 2001.

Pascal, Blaise. *Pascal's Pensées*. Introduction by T. S. Eliot. Project Gutenberg, 2006. http://www.gutenberg.org/files/18269/18269-8.txt/.

Petit, Philippe. *To Reach the Clouds: My High Wire Walk Between the Twin Towers*. New York: North Point, 2002.

Picard, Max. *The World of Silence*. Wichita, KS: Eighth Day Press, 2002.

Pinter, Harold. *Harold Pinter: Complete Works*. Vol. 1. New York: Grove Press, 1976.

Plant, Sadie. *Zeros and Ones: Digital Women and the New Technoculture*. London: Fourth Estate, 1997.

Plath, Sylvia. *The Bell Jar*. Foreword by Frances McCullough. New York: HarperCollins, 1996.

————. *The Collected Poems of Sylvia Plath*. Edited by Ted Hughes. New York: Harper & Row, 1981.

————. *The Unabridged Journals of Sylvia Plath 1950–1962*. Edited by Karen V. Kukil. New York: Anchor Books, 2000.

Platt, Suzy, ed. *Respectfully Quoted: A Dictionary of Quotations*. New York: Barnes & Noble Books, 1993.

Play It Again, Sam. Written by Woody Allen. Directed by Herbert Ross. Hollywood, CA: Paramount Pictures, 1972.

Poe, Edgar Allan. "MS. Found in a Bottle." In *Complete Tales and Poems of Edgar Allan Poe*. New York: Vintage, 1975.

Pope, Alexander. "An Essay on Criticism." In *Essay on Man and Other Poems*. Mineola, NY: Dover Publications, 1994.

Porchia, Antonio. *Voices*. Translated by M. S. Merwin. New York: Alfred A. Knopf, 1988.

Potok, Chaim. *The Chosen*. New York: Ballantine Books, 1982.

Preuss, Paul. "Dark Energy Fills the Cosmos." *Berkeley Lab Research Review*, June 1, 1999.

Proust, Marcel. "In Search of Lost Time." In *Swann's Way*. Translated by C. K. Scott Moncrieff and Terence Kilmartin. Revised by D. J. Enright. Vol. 1. New York: Modern Library, 1998.

Pynchon, Thomas. *Slow Learner*. New York: Little, Brown and Company, 1984.

Rand, Ayn. *Atlas Shrugged*. Centennial ed. New York: Dutton, 2005.

Reid, Constance. *From Zero to Infinity: What Makes Numbers Interesting*. Wellesley, MA: A K Peters, 2006.

Reinhardt, Ad. *Art as Art: The Selected Writings of Ad Reinhardt*. Edited by Barbara Rose. Berkeley: University of California Press, 1991.

Rényi, Alfréd. *Dialogues on Mathematics*. San Francisco: Holden-Day, 1967.

Richard, Paul. "Andy Warhol: A Telling Eye on the Empty." *Washington Post*, February 23, 1987, D1.

Richter, Gerhard. *The Daily Practice of Painting: Writings and*

Interviews 1962–1993. London: Thames & Hudson, 1995.

Rilke, Rainer Maria. *Letters to a Young Poet*. Translated and foreword by Stephen Mitchell. New York: Vintage, 1986.

———. *Rilke's Book of Hours: Love Poems to God*. Translated by Anita Barrows and Joanna Macy. New York: Riverhead Books, 1996.

Robb, Graham. *Balzac: A Biography*. New York: W. W. Norton, 1996.

Roberts, Kate Louise. *Hoyt's New Cyclopedia of Practical Quotations*. New York: Funk & Wagnalls, 1923.

Robinson, Edwin Arlington. *The Man against the Sky: A Book of Poems*. New York: Macmillan Publishing, 1921.

Rodriguez, Jose. Statement made in middle school class as recounted by Nellie Perera, New York, 2002.

Roget's International Thesaurus: The Complete Book of Synonyms and Antonyms. New York: Thomas Y. Crowell, 1946.

Root of All Evil. "Donald Trump vs. Viagra." Episode 1–2, Comedy Central. First broadcast on March 19, 2008.

Rousseau, Jean-Jacques. *The Social Contract*. Translated by Maurice Cranston. New York: Penguin, 1968.

Rumi. *The Essential Rumi*. Translated by Coleman Barks with John Moyne. New York: HarperCollins, 1996.

———. *One-Handed Basket Weaving*. Translated by Coleman Barks. Athens, GA: Mypop, 1991.

———. *Say Nothing: Poems of Jalal al-Din Rumi in Persian and*

English. Translated by Iraj Anvar and Anne Twitty. Sandpoint, ID: Morning Light Press, 2008.

———. *A Year with Rumi: Daily Readings*. Translated by Coleman Barks. New York: HarperCollins, 2006.

Rumsfeld, Donald. Defense Department briefing, Pentagon, Washington, DC, February 12, 2002.

Ryan, Kay. "Nothing Ventured." In *Say Uncle*. New York: Grove Press, 1991.

Sabino, Fernando. *A Time to Meet*. London: Souvenir Press, 1967.

Sabrina. Written by Ernest Lehman, Samuel A. Taylor, and Billy Wilder. Directed by Billy Wilder. Hollywood, CA: Paramount Pictures, 1954.

Saint-Exupéry, Antoine de. *The Little Prince*. Hertfordshire, UK: Wordsworth Editions, 1995.

———. *The Wisdom of the Sands*. Translated by Stuart Gilbert. Chicago: University of Chicago Press, 1979.

Sandburg, Carl. "Anywhere and Everywhere People." In *The Complete Poems of Carl Sandburg*. Revised and expanded ed. New York: Harcourt, 2003.

———. *The People, Yes*. New York: Harvest Books, 1990.

Sangharakshita. *What Is the Dharma? The Essential Teachings of the Buddha*. Birmingham, UK: Windhorse Publications, 1998.

Santayana, George. *Interpretations of Poetry and Religion*. New York: Charles Scribner's Sons, 1921.

Sarton, May. "Where Dreams Begin." In *In Time Like Air: Poems*. New York: Rinehart & Company, 1958.

Sartre, Jean-Paul. *Being and Nothingness*. Translated by Hazel E. Barnes. New York: Citadel Press, 2001.

———. *The Devil and the Good Lord and Two Other Plays*. New York: Alfred A. Knopf, 1960.

Schine, Cathleen. "Romancing the Cosmos." *Vogue*, January 1986.

Scott-Maxwell, Florida. *The Measure of My Days*. New York: Penguin, 1979.

Segoe, Kensaku. *Go Proverbs Illustrated*. Translated by John Bauer. Tokyo: Japanese Go Association, 1960.

Seife, Charles. *Zero: The Biography of a Dangerous Idea*. New York: Viking, 2000.

Seinfeld. "The Pitch." Episode 4-3, NBC. Written by Larry David. First broadcast on September 16, 1992.

Seinfeld, Jerry. Appearance on *Late Show with David Letterman*. Quoted in "Jerry Seinfeld Discusses Career and New Movie 'Bee Movie.'" Interview by Dave Davies. *Fresh Air*, NPR, April 25, 2008.

The Seven Year Itch. Written by Billy Wilder and George Axelrod. Directed by Billy Wilder. Hollywood, CA: Twentieth Century Fox, 1955.

The Shakers. Directed by Ken Burns and Amy Stechler Burns. Florentine Films, 1989.

Shakespeare, William. *Hamlet: Prince of Denmark*. New York: Useful Knowledge Publishing Company, 1882.

———. *King Henry V*. Edited by Richard Grant White. Boston: Houghton, Mifflin and Company, 1883.

———. *King Lear*. Edited by Barbara A. Mowatt and Paul Werstine. New York: Washington Square Press, 1993.

———. *The Merchant of Venice*. Edited by Harry Morgan Ayres. New York: Macmillan Company, 1911.

———. *A Midsummer Night's Dream*. Edited by Sarah Willard Hiestand. Boston: D. C. Heath & Company, 1900.

———. *The Tragedy of King Richard II*. Edited by W. G. Clark, M. A. Oxford: Clarendon Press, 1876.

———. *The Tragedy of Macbeth*. Edited by E. K. Chambers and revised by Edward A. Allen. Boston: D. C. Heath & Company, 1915.

———. *The Winter's Tale*. Edited by Frederick E. Pierce. New Haven, CT: Yale University Press, 1918.

———. *The Works of Shakespeare: Cymbeline*. Edited by Edward Dowden. London: Methuen & Co., 1903.

———. *The Works of Shakespeare: Timon of Athens*. Edited by K. Deighton. London: Methuen & Co., 1905.

Shapiro, Fred R., ed. *The Yale Book of Quotations*. New Haven, CT: Yale University Press, 2006.

Shapiro, Nat, and Nat Hentoff. *Hear Me Talkin' To Ya: The Story of Jazz as Told By the Men Who Made It*. New York: Rinehart, 1955.

Shaw, George Bernard. *Bernard Shaw: Collected Letters 1911–1925*. Edited by Dan H. Laurence. Vol. 3. New York: Viking, 1985.

———. "Too True to be Good." In *Bernard Shaw's Plays*,

edited by Warren Sylvester Smith. New York: W. W. Norton, 1970.

Shelley, Percy Bysshe. "Julian and Maddalo." In *The Selected Poetry and Prose of Shelley*. Hertfordshire, UK: Wordsworth Editions, 1994.

Simic, Charles. "The Hearse." In *The Voice at 3:00 AM: Selected Late and New Poems*. New York: Harcourt, 2003.

Simon, Paul. "The Sound of Silence." *Lyrics: 1964–2008*. New York: Simon & Schuster, 2008.

Singer, Mark. "Predilections." *New Yorker*, February 2, 1989.

Smith, Roberta. "Public Art, Eyesores to Eye Candy." *New York Times*, August 22, 2008, New York ed., AR1.

Smithson, Robert. *The Writings of Robert Smithson*. Edited by Nancy Holt. New York: New York University Press, 1979.

Sontag, Susan. "The Aesthetics of Silence." In *A Susan Sontag Reader*, introduction by Elizabeth Hardwick. New York: Farrar, Straus and Giroux, 1982.

Stardust Memories. Written and directed by Woody Allen. Hollywood, CA: United Artists, 1980.

Stein, Gertrude. *Everybody's Autobiography*. Cambridge, MA: Exact Change, 1993.

———. *The Geographical History of America*. New York: Vintage, 1973.

Stenger, Victor J. *Physics and Psychics*. Amherst, NY: Prometheus Books, 1990.

Stevens, Wallace. *The Collected Poems of Wallace Stevens*. New York: Alfred A. Knopf, 1964.

Stich, Sidra. *Yves Klein.* Stuttgart: Cantz Verlag, 1994.

Stoppard, Tom. *Rosencrantz and Guildenstern Are Dead.* New York: Grove Press, 1967.

Story, William Wetmore. *Poems.* Vol. 2. Boston: Houghton Mifflin, 1886.

Sultan, Stanley. *Eliot, Joyce, and Company.* New York: Oxford University Press, 1987.

Swainson, Bill, ed. *Encarta Book of Quotations.* New York: St. Martin's Press, 2000.

Talking Heads. "Heaven." *Fear of Music.* Written by David Byrne and Jerry Harrison. Burbank, CA: Warner Brothers, 1979.

Tartt, Donna. *The Secret History.* New York: Alfred A. Knopf, 1992.

Tarver, John Charles. *Gustave Flaubert as Seen in His Works and Correspondence.* Edinburgh: Archibald Constable, 1895.

Taylor, Benjamin. *Into the Open: Reflections on Genius and Modernity.* New York: New York University Press, 1995.

Tennyson, Alfred, Lord. *The Works of Tennyson.* New York: Macmillan, 1913.

Thackeray, William Makepeace. *Vanity Fair: A Novel Without a Hero.* London: Thomas Nelson and Sons, 1906.

Thomson, Rupert. *The Book of Revelation.* London: Bloomsbury, 1999.

Thoreau, Henry David. *A Week on the Concord and Merrimack Rivers.* Edited by Odell Shepard. New York: Charles Scribner's Sons, 1921.

———. "Winter: From the Journal of Henry David Thoreau." In *The Writings of Henry David Thoreau*. Vol. 8. Boston: Houghton Mifflin, 1887.

Tillich, Paul. *The Courage to Be*. Introduction by Peter J. Gomes. 2nd ed. New Haven, CT: Yale University Press, 2000.

Tolkien, J. R. R. *The Lord of the Rings*. London: Harper-Collins, 2004.

Tolle, Eckhart. *The Power of Now*. Novato, CA: New World Library, 2004.

Tolstoy, Leo. *War and Peace*. Translated by Nathan Haskell Dole. T. Y. Crowell & Co., 1889.

Torres, Alissa. *American Widow*. Illustrated by Sungyoon Choi. New York: Villard, 2008.

Tracy, Kathleen. *Ellen: The Real Story of Ellen DeGeneres*. New York: Pinnacle Books, 2005.

Tumulty, Joseph P. *Woodrow Wilson as I Know Him*. Garden City, NY: Doubleday, Page, 1921.

Turan, Kenneth. Review of *Into Great Silence*. *Morning Edition*, NPR, March 9, 2007.

Turgenev, Ivan. *Fathers and Sons*. Translated by Rosemary Edmonds. London: Folio Society, 1979.

———. *Fathers and Sons*. Hertfordshire, UK: Wordsworth Editions, 1996.

Twain, Mark. *The Mysterious Stranger and Other Stories*. Afterword by Howard Mittelmark. New York: Signet Classics, 2004.

Updike, John. *Roger's Version*. New York: Fawcett Columbine, 1986.

———. *Self-Consciousness: Memoirs*. New York: Alfred A. Knopf, 1989.

Urish, Ben, and Ken Bielen. *The Words and Music of John Lennon*. Westport, CT: Greenwood Publishing Group, 2007.

van Gogh, Vincent. *Dear Theo: The Autobiography of Vincent van Gogh*. Edited by Irving Stone. Boston: Houghton Mifflin, 1937.

Voltaire. *A Philosophical Dictionary*. 2 vols. London: W. Dugdale, 1843.

Walsh, Timothy. *The Dark Matter of Words*. Carbondale, IL: Southern Illinois University Press, 1998.

Warhol, Andy. "Andy Warhol: My True Story." Interview by Gretchen Berg. In *I'll Be Your Mirror: The Selected Warhol Interviews 1962–1987*, edited by Kenneth Goldsmith. New York: Carroll & Graf Publishers, 2004.

———. *The Philosophy of Andy Warhol (From A to B and Back Again)*. New York: Harcourt, 1977.

Watterson, Bill. *The Authoritative Calvin and Hobbes: A Calvin and Hobbes Treasury*. Kansas City, KS: Andrews and McMeel, 1990.

Watts, Alan. *Buddhism: The Religion of No-Religion*. Boston: Charles E. Tuttle, 1999.

———. *The Essential Alan Watts*. Berkeley, CA: Celestial Arts, 1977.

———. "Meditation." In *The Essential Alan Watts* video series. Produced by Mark Watts. Electronic University, 1977.

———. *Nothingness: The Essence of Alan Watts*. Millbrae, CA: Celestial Arts, 1974.

Weil, Simone. *The Notebooks of Simone Weil*. London: Routledge, 2004.

Whitehead, Alfred North. *An Introduction to Mathematics*. New York: Henry Holt, 1911.

Wideman, John Edgar. "In Praise of Silence." *Callaloo* 22, no. 3 (Summer 1999): 546–49.

Wiesel, Elie. *Elie Wiesel: Conversations*. Edited by Robert Franciosi. Jackson: University Press of Mississippi, 2002.

Wilczek, Frank. "The Persistence of Ether." *Physics Today* 52, no. 1 (January 1999): 11–13.

Wilde, Oscar. "The Critic as Artist." In *Intentions*. New York: Brentano's, 1905.

———. "An Ideal Husband." In *The Importance of Being Earnest and Other Plays*. Edited by Richard Allen Cave. London: Penguin, 2000.

Wilhelm, Kate. "Mrs. Bagley Goes to Mars." In *Somerset Dreams and Other Fictions*. New York: Harper & Row, 1978.

Williams, Tennessee. *Cat on a Hot Tin Roof*. Introduction by Edward Albee. New York: New Directions Publishing, 2004.

Wilmot, John. "Upon Nothing." In *Selected Works*. New York: Penguin, 2004.

Wright, Steven. *Stephen Wright: When the Leaves Blow Away*, Comedy Central. First broadcast on October 21, 2006.

Yeats, William Butler. "Long-legged Fly." In *Yeats's Poetry, Drama, and Prose*, edited by James Pethica. New York: W. W. Norton, 2000.

Yglesias, Rafael. *Fearless*. New York: Warner Books, 1993.

INDEX

ANTONIONI, MICHELANGELO (1912–2007), Italian film director: 175

ARP, HANS (1886–1966), German-French artist and poet: 60

ARTAUD, ANTONIN (1896–1948), French playwright, poet, actor, and theoretician of the theater: 54

AUDEN, W. H. (Wystan Hugh) (1907–1973), English-born US poet: 102

AUSTEN, JANE (1775–1817), English novelist: 135

AUSTER, PAUL (b. 1947–), US novelist: 68, 87, 142, 244

AZRIEL, OF GERONA (13th century), Spanish Jewish mystic: 81

BACON, FRANCIS (1909–1992), Irish-born English painter: 176

BADIOU, ALAIN (b. 1937–), Moroccan-born French philosopher and professor: 27

BALDWIN, JAMES (1924–1987), US novelist and essayist: 87

BALZAC, HONORÉ de (1799–1850), French novelist and playwright: 200

BARENBOIM, DANIEL (b. 1942–), Argentine-born Israeli pianist and conductor: 124

BARRETT, WILLIAM (1913–1992), US philosopher, professor, and critic: 60, 164, 247

BARROW, JOHN D. (b. 1952–), English mathematician, theoretical physicist, and cosmologist: 155, 162, 165

BATAILLE, GEORGES (1897–1962), French librarian, theorist of poststructuralism, and writer: 134

BAUDELAIRE, CHARLES (1821–1867), French critic, poet, and translator: 246

BAUDRILLARD, JEAN (1929–2007), French philosopher, sociologist, and photographer: 198

BECKETT, SAMUEL (1906–1989), Irish playwright, author, and poet: 43, 90–92, 137, 197, 216, 251

BEHAN, BRENDAN (1923–1964), Irish playwright, novelist, and poet: 202

BELLOC, HILAIRE (Joseph Hilaire Pierre) (1870–1953), French-born English writer and historian: 29, 197, 243, 257

BÉNABOU, MARCEL (b. 1939–), Moroccan-born French professor of ancient history and author of postmodern novels: 88

BENNETT, VICTOR (data unknown), English music scholar: 81, 120, 163

BERGSON, HENRI (1859–1941), French philosopher, awarded Nobel Prize in Literature, 1927: 152

BERRY, WENDELL (b. 1934–), US poet, author, critic, and farmer: 185

BIERCE, AMBROSE (Gwinett) (1842–ca. 1914), US journalist and author: 80, 82

BILLINGS, JOSH (Henry Wheeler Shaw) (1818–1885), US humorist and lecturer: 134

BLANCHOT, MAURICE (1907–2003), French writer, literary theorist, and philosopher: 28, 155, 228

BLOFELD, JOHN (1913–1987), English writer, translator, and scholar of Taoism and Chinese Buddhism: 158

BOEHME, JACOB (1575–1624), German Christian mystic and theologian: 214

BOLT, ROBERT (1924–1995), English playwright and screenwriter: 122

BOUNOURE, GABRIEL (1896–1969), French essayist, literary critic, and educator: 43

BRAHMAGUPTA (CE 598–ca. 670), Indian mathematician and astronomer: 141

CHUANG TZU (ca. 369–286 BCE), Chinese philosopher: 34, 48, 158, 219

CHURCHILL, WINSTON (1874–1965), English statesman and writer, awarded Nobel Prize in Literature, 1953: 55, 226

CIORAN, E. M. (Emil Mihai) (1911–1995), Romanian-born French philosopher and essayist: 28, 93–94, 108, 158, 208

CLARKE, ARTHUR C. (1917–2008), English science fiction writer: 227

COHEN, LEONARD (b. 1934–), Canadian musician, songwriter, poet, and novelist: 245

COLE, DICK (b. 1927–), US watercolorist and illustrator: 250

COLE, K. C. (b. 1946–), science writer and professor: 36, 140, 149

COLERIDGE, SAMUEL TAYLOR (1772–1834), English poet, philosopher, and critic: 105

COLLIS, JOHN STEWART (1900–1984), Irish ecologist and author: 150

COLTON, CHARLES CALEB (ca. 1780–1832), English clergyman and writer: 52

CONFUCIUS (551–479 BCE), Chinese philosopher: 134

COOPER, DAVID A. (b. 1939–), US rabbi and teacher of Jewish meditation: 80–81

CRASHAW, RICHARD (ca. 1613–1649), English poet and scholar: 207

CROCKETT, INGRAM (1856–1936), US poet and author: 42

CUNNINGHAM, CONOR (b. 1972–), Irish philosopher and theologian: 188

DAHLBERG, EDWARD (1900–1977), US author, poet, and critic: 234

DANCHEV, ALEX (b. 1955–), English professor, biographer, and essayist: 173

EPICURUS (ca. 341–ca. 270 BCE), Greek philosopher: 158, 195

ERHARD, WERNER (John Paul Rosenberg) (b. 1935–), writer and founder of "est Training": 184

FADIMAN, CLIFTON (1904–1999), US writer and radio and television host: 167

FARADAY, MICHAEL (1791–1867), English chemist, physicist, and inventor: 256

FAULKNER, WILLIAM (1897–1962), US author, awarded Nobel Prize in Literature, 1949: 65

FEYNMAN, RICHARD P. (1918–1988), US physicist, awarded Nobel Prize in Physics, 1965: 111

FIELDING, HENRY (1707–1754), English novelist and playwright: 29, 52, 66, 85, 114, 207, 238

FINN, CHARLES C. (b. 1941–), US writer and professional counselor: 164

FISCHER, NORMAN (b. ca. 1946–), US Buddhist priest, writer, and poet: 218

FLAUBERT, GUSTAVE (1821–1880), French novelist: 72, 88, 205, 242, 247

FRANKLIN, BENJAMIN (1706–1790), US statesman, scientist, and writer: 115, 213

FROST, ROBERT (1874–1963), US poet: 249

GARDNER, MARTIN (b. 1914–), US logician and mathematics and science writer: 200

GENZ, HENNING (b. 1938–), German physicist and author: 79

GENZLINGER, NEIL (b. 1954–), US arts editor, critic, and playwright: 167

GERSHWIN, IRA (1896–1983), US lyricist: 238

GILBERT, ELIZABETH (b. 1969–), US author and biographer: 167

GILBERT, W. S. (William Schwenck) (1836–1911), English playwright, poet, librettist, and illustrator: 223

GILOT, FRANÇOISE (Marie Françoise) (b. 1921–), French-born US painter and author: 220

GINSBERG, ALLEN (1926–1997), US poet: 58

GIULIANI, RUDOLPH (b. 1944–), US lawyer, politician, and businessman: 224

GOULD, CLAUDIA (b. 1956–), US museum director and curator: 66

GRIFFITHS, PAUL (b. 1947–), Welsh-born English new music historian, librettist, critic, and author: 124, 158

GROTSTEIN, JAMES S. (b. 1925–), US psychiatrist and clinical professor: 80, 107

GUERICKE, OTTO VON (1602–1686) German scientist, inventor, and politician: 28, 209

GUSDORF, GEORGES (1912–2000), French philosopher and epistemologist: 125

GUTHRIE, WOODY (Woodrow Wilson) (1912–1967), US folk musician and singer-songwriter: 37

ha-LAVAN, DAVID ben ABRAHAM (ca. late 13th–early 14th century), rabbi and Kabbalist thinker: 28

HAMILTON, WILLIAM (b. 1939–), US cartoonist, playwright, and author: 236

HANDY, W. C. (1873–1958), blues musician and composer: 124

HARDISON, O. B., JR. (Osborne) (1928–1990), US writer, poet, educator, and director of the Folger Shakespeare Library, Theater, and Consort: 147

HARDY, THOMAS (1840–1928), English novelist and poet: 129

HARRISON, JERRY (Jeremiah Griffin Harrison) (b. 1949–), US songwriter, musician, and producer: 137, 253

HAWKING, STEPHEN (WILLIAM) (b. 1942–), English theoretical physicist, mathematician, and author: 148–49

HEART SUTRA: Mahāyāna Buddhist sutra, from the Perfection of Wisdom texts: 57

HEATH, P. L. (1920–2002), Italian-born English philosopher and professor: 54, 78, 155

HEGEL, GEORG WILHELM FRIEDRICH (1770–1831), German philosopher: 79, 217, 250

HEIDEGGER, MARTIN (1889–1976), German philosopher: 78, 107, 114, 150, 163, 169, 235

HELLENGA, ROBERT (b. 1941–), US novelist: 125

HELLMAN, LILLIAN (1905–1984), US playwright: 65, 229

HEMINGWAY, ERNEST (1899–1961), US novelist, awarded Nobel Prize in Literature, 1954: 39, 246

HENRY, GARY (b. 1950–), US clergyman and writer: 212

HERBERT, FRANK (Franklin Patrick) (1920–1986), US science fiction writer: 40

HESCHEL, ABRAHAM JOSHUA (1907–1972), Polish-born US rabbi and leading Jewish theologian: 121, 208

HEYWARD, DuBOSE (1885–1940), US novelist, dramatist, and poet: 238

HITCHCOCK, ALFRED (1899–1980), English filmmaker and producer: 196

HOFFER, ERIC (1902–1983), US labor leader and writer: 181

HOLT, JIM (b. 1954–), US writer and book critic: 229

HOMER (ca. 8th century BCE), Greek (Ionian) poet: 51

HUBBARD, ELBERT (1856–1915), US writer, publisher, and artist: 82

HUGHES, TED (1930–1998), English poet: 228

MORE, HANNAH (1745–1833), English religious writer and philanthropist: 53

MORRIS, ERROL (b. 1948–), US filmmaker and documentarian: 145

MORRISON, VAN (George Ivan) (b. 1945–), Irish musician and poet: 126

MOTHER MEERA (Kamala Reddy) (b. 1960–), Indian-born German spiritual leader: 128

MOTHER TERESA (Agnesë Gonxhe Bojaxhiu) (1910–1997), Albanian-born Indian Roman Catholic nun, awarded Nobel Peace Prize, 1979: 208

NABOKOV, VLADIMIR (1899–1977), Russian-born US novelist: 110

NAIPAUL, V. S. (b. 1932–), Trinidadian-born English writer, awarded Nobel Prize in Literature, 2001: 112

NEEDLEMAN, JACOB (b. 1934–), US philosopher, professor, and writer: 58

NEW TESTAMENT, second later half of the Bible, written ca. CE 100–400: 253

NEWMAN, RANDY (b. 1943–), US musician and songwriter: 109

NIELSEN, LESLIE (b. 1926–), Canadian-born US actor: 230

NIETZSCHE, FRIEDRICH (1844–1900), German philosopher: 110, 159, 216

NIN, ANAÏS (Angela Anaïs Juana Antolina Rosa Edelmira Nin y Culmell) (1903–1977), Catalan-Cuban-French writer: 137

NISHITANI, KEIJI (1900–1990), Japanese philosopher of the Kyoto School: 56, 71

NOVAK, MICHAEL (b. 1933–), US philosopher, theologian, and writer: 208

PINTER, HAROLD (1930–2008), English playwright, awarded Nobel Prize in Literature, 2005: 38, 54, 196–97

PLANT, SADIE (b. 1964–), English writer and philosopher: 143

PLATH, SYLVIA (1932–1963), US writer and poet: 43, 63, 111, 159

POE, EDGAR ALLAN (1809–1849), US poet, writer, and literary critic: 244

POPE, ALEXANDER (1688–1744), English poet: 105

PORCHIA, ANTONIO (1885–1968), Italian-born Argentine poet: 40, 63, 81, 157, 160, 232

POTOK, CHAIM (1929–2002), US rabbi, editor, and novelist: 126

PROESCH, GILBERT (b. 1943), Italian-born British artist, part of collaborative team Gilbert and George: 201

PROUST, MARCEL (1871–1922), French novelist and critic: 86, 115

PYNCHON, THOMAS (1937–), US novelist: 135

RAND, AYN (Alissa Rosenbaum) (1905–1982), Russian-born US writer: 51

REID, CONSTANCE (b. 1918–), US mathematics writer and biographer: 140

REINHARDT, AD (Fredrick Adolph) (1913–1967), US abstract painter: 179

RÉNYI, ALFRÉD (1921–1970), Hungarian mathematician: 194

RICHTER, GERHARD (b. 1932–), German postwar painter: 153

RILKE, RAINER MARIA (1875–1926), German poet and novelist: 86, 113, 130

RIVAROL, ANTOINE de (Antoine Rivaroli, self-styled comte de Rivarol) (1753–1801), French writer: 225

ROBINSON, EDWIN ARLINGTON (1869–1935), US poet: 111

RODRIGUEZ, JOSE (b. ca. 1989–), student: 151

ROUSSEAU, JEAN-JACQUES (1712–1778), Swiss-born French philosopher, writer, and composer: 71, 113

RUDNICK, LAWRENCE (b. 1952–), US astronomer and professor: 150

RUMI (Mowlana Jalal ad-Din Muhammad Rumi) (1207–1273), Persian poet, professor, and Sufi mystic: 43, 98–99, 183, 185, 209, 252

RUMSFELD, DONALD (b. 1932–), US government official and former Secretary of Defense: 226

RYAN, KAY (b. 1945–), US poet and educator, named 16th poet laureate of the United States, 2008: 105

SABINO, FERNANDO (1923–2004), Brazilian journalist and author: 52, 62

SAINT-EXUPÉRY, ANTOINE de (1900–1944), French author, essayist, and aviator: 181, 219

SALMON, WESLEY (1925–2001), US philosopher and professor: 143

SANDBURG, CARL (1878–1967), US poet: 73, 230, 232, 254

SANGHARAKSHITA (Dennis Lingwood) (b. 1925–), English translator, author, Buddhist monk: 213

SANTAYANA, GEORGE (1863–1952), Spanish-born US philosopher, poet, and critic: 206

SARTON, MAY (1912–1995), Belgian-born US poet and novelist: 103

SARTRE, JEAN-PAUL (1905–1980), French philosopher and writer, awarded Nobel Prize in Literature, 1964: 35, 79, 81, 106, 111, 116, 153, 160, 207

SCHAFFNER, INGRID (b. 1961), US curator and writer: 59, 83, 235, 238

CREDITS AND PERMISSIONS

Grateful acknowledgment is made for permission to reprint the following quotes:

WENDELL BERRY:

Page 185: "Accept what comes from silence..." Wendell Berry from *Given: Poems*, copyright © 2006 by Wendell Berry. Reprinted by permission of Counterpoint.

Ernest Hemingway:

Rodney Jones:

PHILIP LARKIN:

Page 53: "Just think of all the spare time…" Excerpt from "Vers de Société" from *Collected Poems* by Philip Larkin. Copyright © 1988, 2003 by the Estate of Philip Larkin. Reprinted by permission of Farrar, Straus and Giroux, LLC, Faber and Faber Ltd. and the Society of Authors, literary representative of the Estate of Philip Larkin.

THE BEATLES:

Page 231: "He's a real nowhere man…" Lyrics from "Nowhere Man" copyright © 1965 Sony/ATV Tunes LLC. All rights administered by Sony/ATV Music Publishing, 8 Music Square West, Nashville, TN 37203. All rights reserved. Used by permission.

W. S. MERWIN:

Page 69: "Of course there is nothing the matter…" Copyright © 1967 by W. S. Merwin, reprinted with permission of The Wylie Agency LLC.

SYLVIA PLATH:

Page 43: "Simmering…like birth pangs." Five lines from "The Rabbit Catcher." From *The Collected Poems of Sylvia*

Plath, edited by Ted Hughes. Copyright © 1906, 1965, 1971, 1981 by the Estate of Sylvia Plath. Editorial material copyright © 1981 by Ted Hughes. Reprinted by permission of HarperCollins Publishers and Faber and Faber Ltd.

RAINER MARIA RILKE:

Page 86: "We see the brightness of a new page..." "Ich lebe grad.../I'm living just as the century ends." From *Rilke's Book of Hours: Love Poems to God* by Rainer Maria Rilke, translated by Anita Barrows and Joanna Macy. Copyright © 1996 by Anita Barrows and Joanna Macy. Used by permission of the translators and Riverhead Books, an imprint of Penguin Group (USA) Inc.

KAY RYAN:

Page 105: "Nothing exists as a block..." "Nothing Ventured" by Kay Ryan from *Say Uncle*. Copyright © 1991 by Kay Ryan. Used by permission of Grove/Atlantic, Inc.

CARL SANDBURG:

Page 73: "I am zero, naught, one cipher,..." Excerpt from "Section #36" in *The People, Yes*, by Carl Sandburg. Copyright © 1936 by Harcourt, Inc. and renewed 1964 by Carl Sandburg, reprinted by permission of Houghton Mifflin

Harcourt Publishing Company. This material may not be reproduced in any form or by any means without the prior written permission of the publisher.

CHARLES SIMIC:

Page 104: "Everything is made of light..." Excerpt from "The Hearse" in *The Voice at 3:00 AM*. Copyright © 2003 by Charles Simic, reprinted by permission of Houghton Mifflin Harcourt Publishing Company.

PAUL SIMON:

Page 123: "And in the naked light I saw..." Copyright © 1964 Paul Simon. Used by permission of the Publisher: Paul Simon Music.

WALLACE STEVENS:

Page 44: "For the listener...." From "The Snow Man" in *The Collected Poems of Wallace Stevens* by Wallace Stevens. Copyright © 1954 by Wallace Stevens and renewed 1982 by Holly Stevens. Used by permission of Alfred A. Knopf, a division of Random House, Inc. and Faber and Faber, Ltd.

Page 186: "I do not know which to prefer...." From "Thirteen Ways of Looking at a Blackbird" in *The Collected Poems of Wallace Stevens* by Wallace Stevens. Copyright © 1954 by

Wallace Stevens and renewed 1982 by Holly Stevens. Used by permission of Alfred A. Knopf, a division of Random House, Inc. and Faber and Faber, Ltd.

Page 211: "If there must be a god...." From "Less and Less Human, O Savage Spirit" from *The Collected Poems of Wallace Stevens* by Wallace Stevens. Copyright © 1954 by Wallace Stevens and renewed 1982 by Holly Stevens. Used by permission of Alfred A. Knopf, a division of Random House, Inc. and Faber and Faber, Ltd.

CHARLES C. FINN:

Page 164: "I tell you everything...." Excerpt from "Please Hear What I am Not Saying." Copyright © 1966 by Charles Finn. Reprinted by permission of the author.

ABOUT THE AUTHOR

JOAN KONNER conceived and edited *The Atheist's Bible*, which became a national bestseller in 2007. She is a longtime award-winning journalist in television and print. Her most recent television production was *The Mystery of Love*, a two-hour documentary special broadcast on public television in December 2006. She served for nine years as Dean of the Columbia Graduate School of Journalism, where she introduced and taught the course "Covering Ideas." She is now Professor Emerita and Dean Emerita of the School, as well as the former publisher and currently honorary co-chair of the *Columbia Journalism Review*.